# MILITARY AVIATION LIBRARY
## World War II

MILITARY AVIATION LIBRARY
World War II

# Japanese & Italian
# Aircraft

**Bill Gunston**

CHARTWELL
BOOKS, INC.

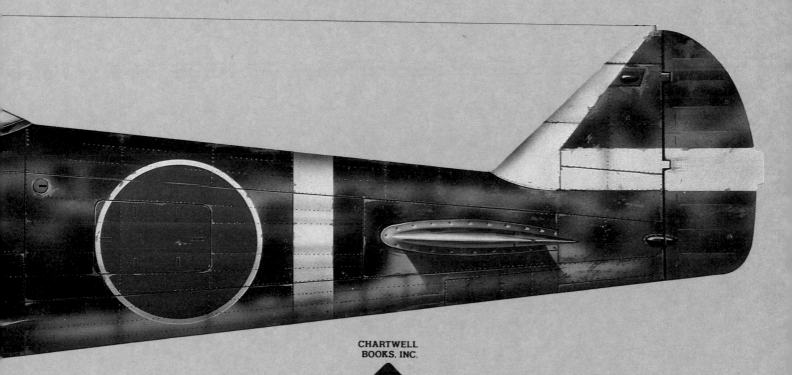

Published by Chartwell Books Inc., New York

**ISBN: 0 89009 899 9**

## PICTURE CREDITS

# Contents

# Italy

# Cant Z.501 Gabbiano

## Z.501 and 501bis Gabbiano (Gull)

**Origin:** CRDA Cantieri Riuniti dell' Adriatico, Monfalcone.
**Type:** Patrol flying boat.
**Engine:** 900hp Isotta-Fraschini Asso XIR2 C15 vee-12 liquid-cooled.
**Dimensions:** Span 73ft 9¾in (22·50m); length (most) 46ft 11in (14·30m); height 14ft 6in (4·42m).
**Weights:** Empty (typical) 8,488lb (3850kg); loaded 13,117lb (5950kg); max overload 15,542lb (7050kg).
**Performance:** Maximum speed 171mph (275km/h); normal range 1,490 miles (2400km); ultimate overload range 3,000 miles (4830km).
**Armament:** Two 7·7mm Breda-SAFAT manually aimed from engine nacelle and dorsal hull cockpit (early versions, third similar gun in bow position); racks on bracing struts for weapon load of 1,404lb (637kg).
**History:** First flight August 1934; service (military) delivery 1936; final delivery, probably late 1942.
**User:** Italy (RA, CB and ARSI); post-war Italian AF.

**Above: A Z.501 Gabbiano of the 46th Squadriglia Ricognizione Marittima. Some examples had enclosed bow cockpits.**

**Development:** It is curious that in World War II Italy should have used a wealth of float seaplanes but only one major type of flying boat. One of Ing Filippo Zappata's earliest designs, the Gabbiano set world class records for non-stop distance in 1934 and 1935, flying from Monfalcone to Eritrea and then to Somaliland. Several civil examples existed when production began for the Regia Aeronautica as a four/five-seat reconnaissance and attack machine, and by the entry into war in June 1940 no fewer than 202 were on strength. At first the 501 was active, but casualties in the face of the enemy were heavy, and attrition of the wooden aircraft severe, and as production slumped the operational force dwindled to about 40 at the September 1943 Armistice. About 19 served with the CB force and a few remained operational with the RSI. Several were still in service in 1950.

# Cant Z.506B Airone

## Z.506B Airone (Heron) serie I-XII and Z.506S

**Origin:** CRDA Cantieri Riuniti dell' Adriatico, Monfalcone; second-source production by Piaggio.
**Type:** Torpedo, bomber and reconnaissance seaplane, (S) air/sea rescue.
**Engines:** Three 750hp Alfa Romeo 126RC34 nine-cylinder radials.
**Dimensions:** Span 86ft 11¼in (26·50m); length 63ft 2in (19·25m); height 24ft 5½in (7·45m).
**Weights:** Empty 19,290lb (8750kg); max loaded 27,997lb (12,700kg).
**Performance:** Maximum speed 217mph (350km/h); typical endurance 6hr 26min; range with 2,094lb (950kg) weapon load 1,243 miles (2000km).
**Armament:** (Typical early series) ventral bay housing 1,764lb (800kg) torpedo or up to 2,205lb (1000kg) bombs or other weapons, with 7·7mm Breda-SAFAT manually aimed from rear, and retractable Breda M.1 dorsal turret with two 12·7mm Breda-SAFAT; (Serie XII) bomb load increased to 2,645lb (1200kg), dorsal turret changed to Delta E with one 12·7mm Scotti, and two 7·7mm Breda-SAFAT from beam windows.
**History:** First flight 1936; service delivery (civil) 1936, (military) December 1937; final delivery not known.
**Users:** Italy (Ala Littoria, RA, CB, ARSI and post-war AF), Germany (Luftwaffe), Poland.

**Development:** In 1936–37 civil Z.506 Airones set 16 world class records for speed, range and payload/height. The military version proved one of the finest marine aircraft ever built, and despite wooden construction was able to operate in Force 5 conditions and survive until at least 1959. Only one reached Poland, three days before the German assault. Italian examples served in Spain, and 95 were on strength in June 1940. In 1940–41

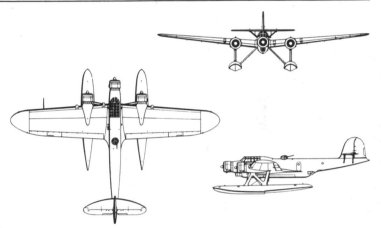

**Above: Three-view of Z.506B Airone. Though less powerful than the Z.1007 landplane bomber (overleaf) the Airone was larger.**

Airones were in hectic action in the Balkans, France and against the Allied navies, but by mid-1941 they were reassigned to coastal patrol, ASW and escort, with the Z.506S (Soccorso) converted for ASR operations. They had an outstanding record, and one achieved fame as the only aircraft ever hijacked by prisoners of war (the RAF took over and flew to Malta).

**Below, left: On its beaching chassis the Airone stood high off the ground, a long ladder being needed to reach even the main entry door on the left side. Their tough utilitarian qualities kept these floatplanes flying up to and beyond the Italian surrender. One remained operational until 1956.**

**Below: About half the Airones of the Regia Aeronautica were painted dark olive (a green-brown) above and pale yellow green below, with the Mediterranean white theatre band. The ladder is not part of the aircraft.**

# Cant Z.1007 Alcione

## Z.1007, 1007 bis and 1018

**Origin:** CRDA "Cant".
**Type:** Four/five-seat medium bomber.
**Engines:** Three 1,000hp Piaggio P.XIbis RC40 14-cylinder two-row radials.
**Dimensions:** Span 81ft 4in (24·8m); length 60ft 4in (18·4m); height 17ft 1½in (5·22m).
**Weights:** Empty 19,000lb (8630kg); loaded 28,260—30,029lb (12,840—13,620kg).
**Performance:** Maximum speed 280mph (448km/h); initial climb 1,550ft (472m)/min; service, ceiling 26,500ft (8100m); range 800 miles (1280km) with maximum bombs, 3,100 miles (4989km) with maximum fuel.
**Armament:** (First 25) four 7·7mm Breda-SAFAT machine guns in dorsal turret, two beam hatches and ventral position; (remainder) as before except dorsal and ventral guns 12·7mm Breda-SAFAT; internal bomb capacity 4,410lb (2000kg); alternatively two 1,000lb (454kg) torpedoes and four bombs up to 551lb (250kg) each on underwing racks.

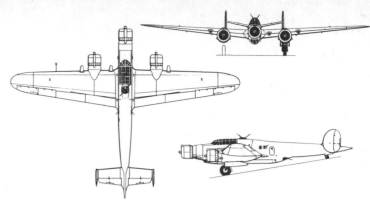

Above: Three-view of typical Z.1007bis (twin-finned version).

Left: A twin-finned Z.1007bis of 230a Squadriglia, 950 Gruppo.

Below: Part of a formation of Z.1007bis (single-fin model, no separate designation) winging their way to a target in the Balkans. Construction was almost entirely of wood.

**History:** First flight May 1937; (first production aircraft) 1939; entry to service 1939.
**User:** Italy (RA, CB, ARSI).

**Development:** A famous Italian naval yard, the Cantieri Monfalcone (Trieste), entered the aircraft construction business in 1923, forming a subsidiary called Cantieri Riuniti dell' Adriatico (always shortened to Cant). Their first products were seaplanes and flying boats and the most important of these was the three-engined Z.506B Airone (Heron) twin-float seaplane used in large numbers in World War II. Designer Filippo Zappata then produced a landplane bomber version, powered by three 840hp Isotta-Fraschini Asso inverted-vee liquid-cooled engines. Like the seaplane this new bomber, the Z.1007, was built entirely of wood. It received a generally favourable report from the Regia Aeronautica's test pilots and after modifications went into production, two other firms — Meridionali and Piaggio — later being brought in to increase rate of output. Nearly all the several hundred production Alciones (Kingfishers) were powered by the Piaggio radial engine, and this version, the Z.1007 bis, also had a longer fuselage, bigger wings and stronger landing gear. Almost·half also had twin tail fins.

Though easy meat for RAF fighters, Alciones were bravely operated throughout the Mediterranean, and many even served on the Russian front. Various developments culminated in the excellent twin-engined Z.1018 Leone (Lion), with metal airframe and 1,350hp engines, but few of these had been delivered when Italy surrendered in 1943.

# Caproni Ca 133

## Ca 101, 111 and 133 (data for 133)

**Origin:** Società Italiana Caproni.
**Type:** Colonial bomber and transport.
**Engines:** Three 450/460hp Piaggio P.VII RC14 Stella seven-cylinder radials.
**Dimensions:** Span 69ft 8in (21·3m); length 50ft 4¾in (15·35m); height 13ft 1in (4m).
**Weights:** Empty 8,598lb (3900kg); loaded 14,330lb (6500kg).
**Performance:** Maximum speed 174mph (280km/h); initial climb 940ft (286m)/min; service ceiling 21,325ft (6500m); range 839 miles (1350km).
**Armament:** One or two 7·7mm or one 12·7mm machine gun on pivoted mounting in roof at trailing edge of wing; one machine gun in sliding hatchway in floor of rear fuselage; often one 7·7mm on each side in aft window-openings; bomb load (up to 2,200lb, 1000kg) carried in internal bay and on external racks under fuselage.
**History:** First flight (Ca 101) 1932; (Ca 111) 1933; (Ca 133) 1935; end of production, prior to 1938.
**Users:** Austria, Hungary, Italy (RA).

**Development:** As Mussolini restored "the lost colonies" and Italy forcibly built up an overseas empire, so did the need arise for "colonial" type aircraft similar to the British Wapiti and Vincent. Caproni produced the Ca 101 to meet this need, at least 200 being delivered in the early 1930s to serve as bomber, troop carrier, reconnaissance and ground attack machines and, most of all, to supply forward troops with urgent stores. Powered by three 235hp Alfa Romeo engines, it was made of robust welded steel tube with fabric covering. The Ca 111, powered by a single 950hp Isotta-Fraschini engine, gave even better service and survived the Albanian and Ethiopian campaigns to operate against Jugoslav partisans in World War II. The Ca 133 was the most important of all and many hundreds were built. When Italy entered the war in 1940 it equipped 14 Squadriglie di Bombardimento Terrestri (bomber squadrons), nearly all in East or North Africa. Though scorned by the RAF and easy meat on the ground or in the air, these versatile STOL machines worked hard and well and finished up as ambulances and transports in Libya, on the Russian Front and in Italy (on both sides after the 1943 surrender).

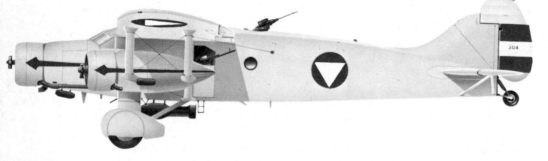

Left: A fully armed Ca 133 of Fliegerregiment 2 of the Austrian Air Force, one of several export customers. In the 1930s these versatile machines gave excellent service, but by the time Italy entered World War II they were outclassed. Their crews called them Vacca (cow) or Caprona (she-goat), which was a play on the name of the manufacturer. Two advanced models, the Ca 142 and 148, did not go into production.

# Caproni Ca 135

## Ca 135 and 135bis (data for 135bis)

**Origin:** Società Italiana Caproni.
**Type:** Five-seat medium bomber.
**Engines:** Two 1,000hp Piaggio P.XIbis RC40 14-cylinder two-row radials.
**Dimensions:** Span 61ft 8in (18·75m); length 47ft 1in (14·4m); height 11ft 2in (3·4m).
**Weights:** Empty 9,921lb (4500kg); loaded 18,740lb (8500kg).
**Performance:** Maximum speed 273mph (440km/h); initial climb 1,435ft (437m)/min; service ceiling 22,966ft (7000m); range with bomb load 746 miles (1200km).
**Armament:** Three Breda-SAFAT turrets, each mounting one 12·7mm or two 7·7mm guns, in nose, dorsal and ventral positions (dorsal and ventral retractable); bomb cells in fuselage and inner wings for up to 3,527lb (1600kg) weapon load.
**History:** First flight (135) 1 April 1935; (135bis) about November 1937.
**Users:** Hungary, Italy (RA).

**Development:** When the great Caproni combine took on Breda's designer Cesare Pallavicino it embarked on a series of modern aircraft of higher performance. The most important appeared to be the Ca 135 medium bomber, designed in the summer of 1934 to meet a Regia Aeronautica specification. A curious blend of wooden wings, light-alloy monocoque forward fuselage and steel tube plus fabric rear fuselage and tail, the prototype had two 800hp Isotta-Fraschini Asso engines but no guns. After over a year of testing the government ordered 14 as the Tipo Spagna to serve in the Spanish civil war. Peru bought six Tipo Peru, eventually purchasing 32. Yet the Ca 135 was not as good as the S.M.79 and Z.1007 by rival makers and the Regia Aeronautica kept delaying a decision. More powerful Fiat A.80 RC41 radials improved behaviour but at the expense of reliability and a good 135 did not appear until the Milan Aero Show in October 1937, when the Piaggio-engined 135bis was displayed. Though never adopted by the Regia Aeronautica it was frequently identified as having been used against Malta, Jugoslavia and Greece! The real raiders in these cases were probably BR.20s, but the 135 bis did find a customer: the Hungarian Air Force. Several hundred were operated by that service whilst attached to Luftflotte IV in the campaign on the Eastern Front in 1941–43.

**Left:** One of the colourful Ca 135bis bombers operated on the Eastern Front by the Hungarian Air Force (note tactical theatre marking of yellow bands). This example belonged to 4/III Bomb Group, but few of the Capronis lasted even until the end of 1942, and they were not entirely successful.

# Caproni Ca 309-316

## Ca 309 Ghibli (Desert Wind), 310 Libeccio (Southwest Wind), 311 and 311M, 312 and variants, 313, 314 and variants and 316

**Origin:** Cantieri Aeronautici Bergamaschi; production by various other Caproni companies, mainly at Castellamare and Taliedo.
**Type:** (309) colonial utility, (310) utility transport, (311) light bomber, (312) bomber and torpedo (312bis, 312IS, seaplanes), (313) bomber/torpedo bomber, (314) coastal patrol torpedo bomber, (316) catapult reconnaissance seaplane.
**Engines:** (309) two 185hp Alfa Romeo A.115 six-in-line; (310, 316) two 470hp Piaggio P.VII C.16 seven-cylinder radials; (311, 312) two 650hp Piaggio P.XVI RC35 nine-cylinder radials; (313, 314) two 650hp Isotta-Fraschini Delta RC35 inverted-vee-12.
**Dimensions:** Span (309-312) 53ft 1¾in (16·20m), (313) 52ft 10½in (16·11m), (314) 54ft 7½in (16·65m), (316) 52ft 2in (15·90m); length (309) 43ft 7½in (13·30m), (311, 313, 314) 38ft 8in (11·79m), (310, 312) 40ft 0½in (12·20m), (316) 42ft 3in (12·88m); height 10ft 8in to 13ft 3in (floatplanes about 16ft 9in) (3·26 to 4·04m, floatplanes 5·10m).
**Weights:** Empty (309) 3,850lb (1746kg), (others) about 7,050lb (3200kg); loaded (309) 6,067lb (2750kg), (others) 10,252–13,580lb (4650–6160kg).
**Performance:** Maximum speed (309) 158mph (254km/h), (others) 227–271mph (365–435km/h) except 316 only 204mph (328km/h).
**Armament:** See text.
**History:** First flight (309) 1936; main production 1938–42.
**Users:** Italy (civil, RA, CB, ARSI, post-war AF), Germany (Luftwaffe), Croatia, Hungary, Jugoslavia, Norway, Spain, Sweden.

**Development:** This diverse family had wooden wings, and fuselages of welded steel tube covered with fabric. The Ghibli was a light multi-role machine for African use, with radio, cameras, light bomb racks and two machine guns (one fixed, one in a dorsal position). The more powerful examples carried up to five 12·7mm and three 7·7mm guns with bomb/torpedo loads up to 1,764lb (800kg). Total production of all models was about 2,400.

**Left:** Another colourful Italian in foreign colours, in this case a Caproni Ca 310 Libeccio of the Norwegian Army Flying Service (Haerens Flyvevåben). This example was based at Sola airfield, Stavanger, in 1940, and was almost certainly destroyed on the ground within the first few hours of the German invasion of Scandinavia on 9 April 1940.

**Above:** A Caproni Ca 312 of the type with an unstepped nose. Most subsequent models reverted to a conventional windscreen.

**Above:** The Ca 310 Libeccio was the first of the family to have retractable landing gear. Later versions were more powerful.

# Fiat B.R.20 Cicogna

## B.R.20, 20M and 20 bis

**Origin:** Aeronautica d'Italia SA Fiat.
**Type:** Heavy bomber, with normal crew of five or six.
**Engines:** (B.R.20) two 1,000hp Fiat A.80 RC41 18-cylinder two-row radials; (B.R.20M) as B.R.20 or two 1,100hp A.80 RC20; (B.R.20bis) two 1,250hp A.82 RC32.
**Dimensions:** Span, 70ft 9in (21·56m); length, (B.R.20) 52ft 9in (16·2m); (B.R.20M, 20bis) 55ft 0in (16·78m); height 15ft 7in (4·75m).
**Weights:** Empty (all), about 14,770lb (6700kg); loaded (B.R.20) 22,046lb (10,000kg); (B.R.20M) 23,038lb (10,450kg).
**Performance:** Maximum speed, (B.R.20) 264mph (425km/h); (B.R.20M) 267mph (430km/h); (B.R.20bis) 292mph (470km/h); initial climb (all) about 902ft (275m)/min; service ceiling, (B.R.20, 20M) 22,145ft (6750m); (B.R.20bis) 26,246ft (8000m); range, (B.R.20, 20M) 1,243 miles (2000km); (B.R.20bis) 1,710 miles (2750km).
**Armament:** (B.R.20) four 7·7mm Breda-SAFAT machine guns in nose turret (one), dorsal turret (two) and manual ventral position; bomb load 3,527lb (1600kg); (B.R.20M) as B.R.20 except nose gun 12·7mm; (B.R.20bis) as B.R.20M with two extra 12·7mm guns manually aimed from lateral blisters; bomb load 5,511lb (2500kg).
**History:** First flight (prototype) 10 February 1936; service delivery, September 1936; first flight (B.R.20M) late 1939; first flight B.R.20bis, December 1941.
**Users:** Hungary, Italy (RA), Japan, Spain, Venezuela.

**Development:** Ing Rosatelli was responsible for a great series of B.R. (Bombardamento Rosatelli) designs from 1919 onwards. Most were powerful single-engined biplanes, but in the mid-1930s he very quickly produced the B.R.20, a large monoplane with stressed-skin construction and other modern refinements. Despite its relative complexity the original aircraft was put into production within six months of the first flight and by the end of 1936 the B.R.20-equipped 13° Stormo was probably the most advanced bomber squadron in the world. Fiat also built two civil B.R.20L record-breakers, and also offered the new bomber for export, soon gaining a valuable order for 85, not from the expected China but from Japan, which needed a powerful bomber to bridge the gap caused by a delay with the Army Ki-21. In June 1937 the B.R.20 figured prominently in the Aviazione Legionaria sent to fight for the Nationalists in Spain and, with the He 111, bore the brunt of their very successful bomber operations. Spain purchased a manufacturing licence, which was not taken up, and purchased at least 25 from Fiat. An additional number were brought by Venezuela. In 1940, when Italy entered World War II, some 250 had been delivered to the Regia Aeronautica, the last 60 being of the strengthened and much more shapely M (Modificato) type. In October 1940 two groups of 37 and 38 of the M model operated against England, but they were hacked down with ease and were recalled in January 1941. During 1942 the B.R.20 began to fade, becoming used for ocean patrol, operational training and bombing where opposition was light. A large force supported the Luftwaffe in Russia, where casualties were heavy. By the Armistice only 81 of all versions were left out of 606 built. The much improved B.R.20bis never even got into bulk production.

**Left: One of the more uncommon Fiat B.R.20 Cicogna bombers was this example from a batch supplied to the Japanese Army in 1937. No fewer than 75 were delivered, seeing action in both the Chinese campaign and World War II. The aircraft illustrated served with the 1st Chutai, 12th Hikosentai. Japanese designation was Yi-shiki.**

# Fiat C.R.32

## C.R.30, 32 and 32bis

**Origin:** Aeronautica d'Italia SA Fiat; built under licence by Hispano Aviaciòn, Spain.
**Type:** Single-seat fighter.
**Engine:** (C.R.30) one 600hp Fiat A.30 vee-12 water-cooled, (C.R.32) one 600hp Fiat A.30 RAbis.
**Dimensions:** Span (C.R. 30) 34ft 5½in (10·45m); (C.R.32) 31ft 2in (9·5m); length (30) 25ft 8¼in (7·83m); (32) 24ft 5½in (7·45m); height (30) 8ft 7½in (2·62m); (32) 7ft 9in (2·4m).
**Weights:** Empty (both) about 3,100lb (1400kg); loaded (both) about 4,150lb (1900kg).
**Performance:** Maximum speed (30) 217mph (350km/h), (32) 233mph (375km/h); initial climb (both) 2,000ft (907m)/min; service ceiling (both) about 29,530ft (9000m); range (30) 528 miles (850km), (32) 466 miles (750km).
**Armament:** (C.R.30) two fixed Breda-SAFAT 7·7mm or 12·7mm machine guns above engine; (C.R.32) two 12·7mm; (C.R.32bis), two 12·7mm above engine and two 7·7mm above lower wings with provision for single 220lb (100kg) or two 110lb bombs.
**History:** First flight (C.R.30) 1932; (C.R.32) August 1933; final delivery, about October 1939.
**Users:** Argentina, China, Hungary, Italy (RA), Paraguay, Spain, Venezuela.

**Development:** In 1923 Ing Celestino Rosatelli supervised his first C.R. (Caccia Rosatelli) fighter. From it stemmed an unbroken line which reached its climax in the 1930s. The C.R.30 offered a considerable jump in performance, for it had much more power without increase in aircraft drag. The lusty Fiat vee-12 drove a metal propeller and was cooled by a prominent circular radiator in a duct in the chin position below the crankcase. The all-metal structure was notable for continuing the scheme of Warren (W-form)

interplane bracing. The tail was also braced and the main gears had large wheel spats. The C.R.32 was a general refinement, built in larger numbers and forming the major part of the Regia Aeronautica fighter force in 1935–40. In August 1936 some were sent to form La Cucaracha squadron fighting for Franco's fighter units. Spain built many under licence as the Hispano HA-132-L Chirri, and more than 150 were exported by Fiat to China, Hungary and South American countries. The nimble little Fiats were compact, robust and highly manoeuvrable and gave impressive displays all over Europe in the hands of the Pattuglie Acrobatiche. Total Fiat output amounted to at least 1,212, the final 500 being mainly four-gun 32bis fighter-bombers and a few 32ter and 32quater versions with small modifications. The Regia Aeronautica did its best with the C.R. 32 until 1942, finally using it for night tactical operations in Greece, Eritrea and Libya.

**Above: The Fiat C.R.32 was the star performer at countless flying displays by Mussolini's flamboyant Regia Aeronautica in the mid-1930s. It was the mount chosen for the Pattuglie Acrobatiche.**

**Left: The C.R.32 used by a leading ace of the Spanish Nationalist (rebel) air force, Comandante Joaquín García Morato. The C.R.32 also equipped the leading unit of the Regia Aeronautica fighting in Spain, the La Cucaracha squadron. But by 1940 it was no longer capable of acting as a front-line dogfighter.**

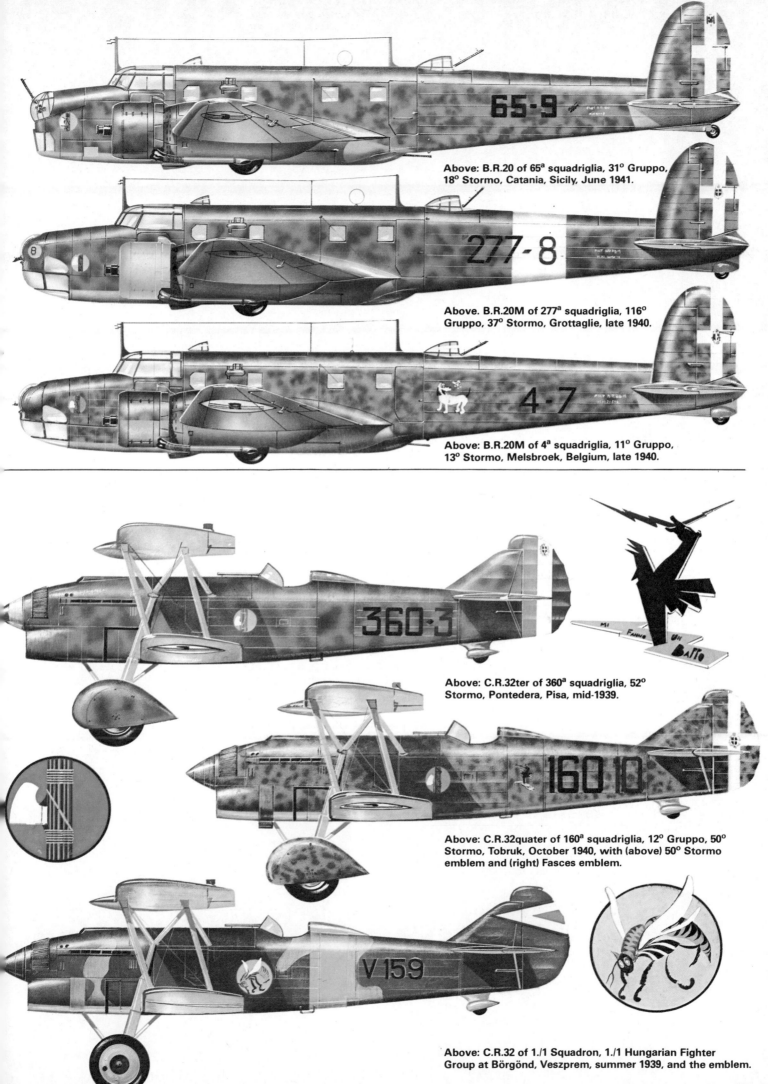

Above: B.R.20 of 65ª squadriglia, 31º Gruppo, 18º Stormo, Catania, Sicily, June 1941.

Above: B.R.20M of 277ª squadriglia, 116º Gruppo, 37º Stormo, Grottaglie, late 1940.

Above: B.R.20M of 4ª squadriglia, 11º Gruppo, 13º Stormo, Melsbroek, Belgium, late 1940.

Above: C.R.32ter of 360ª squadriglia, 52º Stormo, Pontedera, Pisa, mid-1939.

Above: C.R.32quater of 160ª squadriglia, 12º Gruppo, 50º Stormo, Tobruk, October 1940, with (above) 50º Stormo emblem and (right) Fasces emblem.

Above: C.R.32 of 1./1 Squadron, 1./1 Hungarian Fighter Group at Börgönd, Veszprem, summer 1939, and the emblem.

13

# Fiat C.R.42 Falco

## C.R.42, 42bis, 42ter, 42AS and 42N

**Origin:** Aeronautica d'Italia SA Fiat.
**Type:** Single-seat fighter.
**Engine:** One 840hp Fiat A.74 RC38 14-cylinder two-row radial.
**Dimensions:** Span 31ft 10in (9·7m); length 27ft 1¼in (8·25m); height 11ft 0in (3·35m).
**Weights:** Empty 3,790lb (1720kg); loaded 5,070lb (2300kg).
**Performance:** Maximum speed 267mph (430km/h); initial climb 2,400ft (732m)/min; service ceiling 34,450ft (10,500m); range 481 miles (775km).
**Armament:** (Early C.R.42) one 7·7mm and one 12·7mm Breda-SAFAT machine guns mounted above forward fuselage; (C.R.42bis) two 12·7mm; (C.R.42ter) two 12·7mm and two more 12·7mm in fairings beneath lower wing; (C.R.42AS) two/four 12·7mm and underwing racks for two 220lb (100kg) bombs.
**History:** First flight (C.R.41) 1936; (C.R.42) January 1939; first service delivery, November 1939; termination of production, early 1942.
**Users:** Belgium, Finland, Hungary, Italy (RA), Sweden.

**Above: Part of a formation of Fiat C.R.42 Falco fighters of the Regia Aeronautica's 62a Squadriglia. Though outstandingly manoeuvrable, the Falco lacked almost all other fighter qualities.**

**Left: This Falco belonged to the 95a Squadriglia, 10o Gruppo Caccia Terrestre, based at Echeloo, Belgium, in November 1940.**

**Development:** In the mid-1930s the Fiat company made a firm move away from liquid-cooled vee engines and concentrated on air-cooled radials. Rosatelli prepared a fighter, the C.R.41, to take one of these, but only the prototype was built. Other nations were by this time (1936) giving up the open-cockpit, fabric-covered biplane in favour of the stressed-skin monoplane with retractable landing gear, but Rosatelli persisted with his C.R. family and developed the C.R.41 into the C.R.42. Though a robust, clean and very attractive design, it was really obsolete at the time of its first flight. Despite this — and perhaps confirming that Fiat knew the world market — the C.R.42 found ready acceptance. It went into large-scale production for the Regia Aeronautica and for Belgium (34, delivered January–May 1940), Hungary (at least 40, delivered December 1939–June 1940) and Sweden (72, delivered 1940–41). Total production, including the AS close support and N night fighter versions, amounted to 1,784. One group of 50 C.R.42bis provided the fighter element of the Corpo Aereo Italiano which operated from Belgium against England in October 1940–January 1941– with conspicuous lack of success. The rest persevered in the Mediterranean and North African areas, acting as both fighters and ground attack aircraft, a few being converted as dual trainers. One was built in 1940 as a twin-float seaplane and the final fling was a C.R.42B with 1,010hp DB 601A inverted-vee engine. The German power unit made it, at 323mph, the fastest biplane fighter but no production was attempted.

**Right: C.R.42 of 377ª squadriglia autonoma, Palermo-Boccadifalco, Sicily, summer 1942, and (below right) the squadriglia emblem (left) and House of Savoy coat of arms.**

**Below: C.R.42 of 20ª squadriglia, 46º Gruppo Assalto, 15º Stormo on the El Alamein front, September-November 1942.**

**Bottom: C.R.42 of auxiliary assault group, Ravenna area, 1942.**

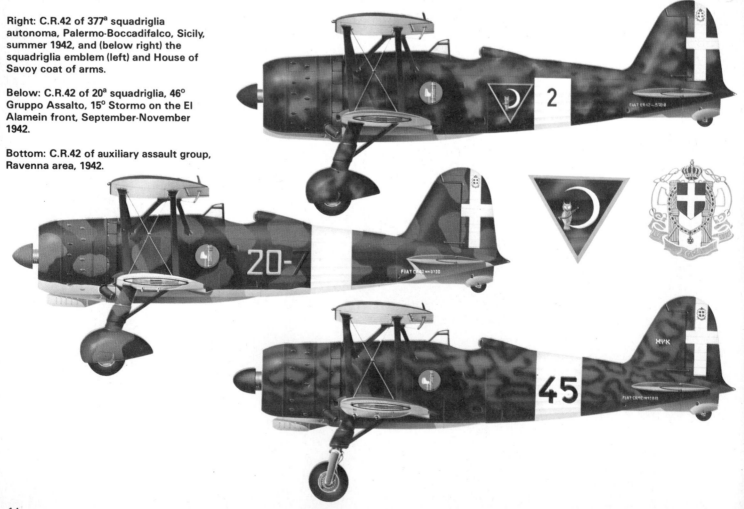

# Fiat G.50 Freccia

## G.50, 50bis, 50ter and 55 Centauro

**Origin:** Aeronautica d'Italia SA Fiat; also built by CMASA.
**Type:** Single-seat fighter.
**Engine:** (G.50, G.50bis) one 840hp Fiat A.74 RC38 14-cylinder two-row radial; (G.50ter) 1,000hp A.76 RC40S; (G.55) 1,475hp Daimler-Benz DB 605A inverted-vee-12 liquid-cooled.
**Dimensions:** Span, (G.50) 36ft 0in (10·97m); (G.55) 38ft 10½in (11·85m); length, (G.50) 25ft 7in (7·79m); (G.55) 30ft 9in (9.37m); height (G.50) 9ft 8in (2·9m); (G.55) 10ft 3¼in (3·15m).
**Weights:** Empty (G.50) 4,188lb (1900kg); (G.55) 6,393lb (2900kg); loaded (G.50) 5,966lb (2706kg); (G.55) 8,179lb (3710kg).
**Performance:** Maximum speed (G.50) 293mph (471km/h); (G.55) 385mph (620km/h); initial climb (G.50) 2,400ft (731m)/min; (G.55) 3,300ft (1000m)/min; service ceiling (G.50) 32,810ft (10,000m); (G.55) 42,650ft (13,000m); range (G.50) 621 miles (1000km); (G.55) 994 miles (1600km).
**Armament:** (G.50, G.50bis) two 12·7mm Breda-SAFAT machine guns above front fuselage; (G.55/0) as above, plus one 20mm Mauser MG 151 cannon firing through propeller hub; (G.55/I) as G.55/0 plus two 20mm MG 151 in outer wings.
**History:** First flight 26 February 1937; (G.50bis) September 1940; (G.55) 30 April 1942.
**Users:** Finland, Italy (RA, CB, ARSI), Spain.

**Development:** In 1935 the issue of a specification for an all-metal monoplane fighter for the Regia Aeronautica attracted at least six competing designs. Though the Macchi 200 was ultimately to become dominant, the initial winner was the Fiat G.50, the first major design by Ing Giuseppe Gabrielli (hence the designation). Its flight trials went smoothly, an order was placed in September 1937 for 45 and deliveries began early in 1938. About a dozen of the first production G.50s were sent to reinforce the Aviazione Legionaria in Spain, where their good qualities of speed and manoeuvrability were manifest. On the other hand pilots disliked having a

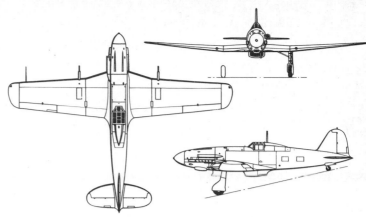

**Above: Three-view of the G.55/I with three cannon.**

sliding cockpit canopy, which was not easy to open quickly and interfered with vision, and in the next production batch of 200 an open cockpit was adopted. The poor armament was not changed, but fairings for the retracted wheels were added. Production from the CMASA plant at Marina di Pisa got under way in 1939, with deliveries replacing the C.R.32 in Regia Aeronautica fighter squadrons (not always to the pilots' delight), and a further 35 being flown to Finland in 1940 where they gave admirable service. The main production version was the G.50bis, with reprofiled fuselage giving improved pilot view, armour and self-sealing tanks. About 450 were built, mainly by CMASA. Other versions included the tandem-seat G.50B trainer, of which 139 were built; the G.50ter with more powerful engine; and proto-types of the G.50bis-A, with four 12·7mm guns and racks for two bombs, and of the DB 601A-powered G.50V. Few G.55 were built.

**Right: G.50 of Grupo Num 27, Regimiento Mixto de Africa, Spanish EdA, Melilla, Morocco, March 1940, and (below right) the Grupo's emblem.**

**Below: G.50bis Scuola Caccia 11° Periodo, Regia Aeronautica, in the summer of 1942.**

**Below centre: G.50bis of 20° Gruppo, Ursel, Belgium, from October 1940.**

**Bottom: G.50 in Finnish service.**

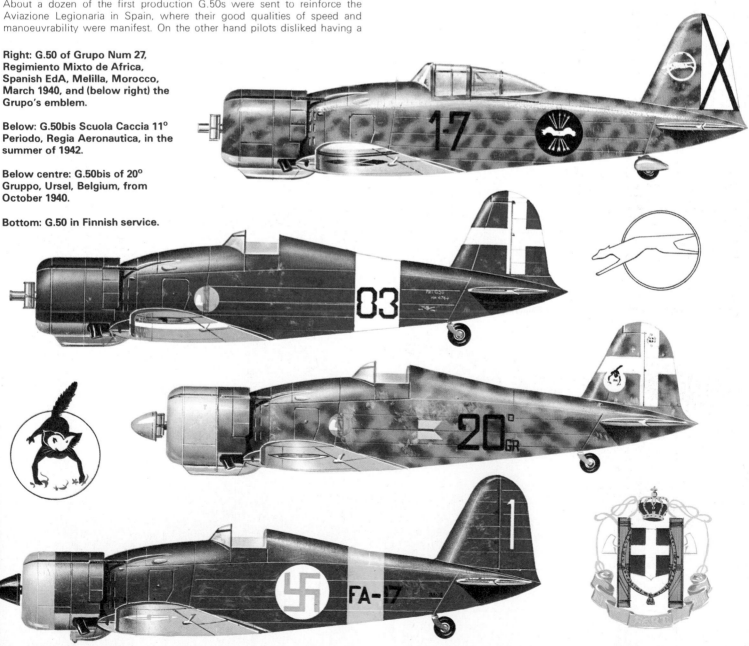

15

# Macchi M.C. 200 Saetta

## M.C.200 (Serie I-XXI) and M.C.201

**Origin:** Aeronautica Macchi.
**Type:** Single-seat day fighter.
**Engine:** One 870hp Fiat A74RC38 14-cylinder two-row radial.
**Dimensions:** Span 34ft 8½in (10·58m); length 26ft 10½in (8·2m); height 11ft 6in (3·38m).
**Weights:** (Typical) empty 4,188lb (1900kg); (prototype) 3,902lb; (final production Serie XXI) 4,451lb; loaded 5,182lb (2350kg); (prototype) 4,850lb; (Serie XXI) 5,598lb.
**Performance:** Maximum speed 312mph (501km/h); initial climb 3,215ft (980m)/min; service ceiling 29,200ft (8900m); range 354 miles (570km).
**Armament:** Two 12·7mm Breda-SAFAT machine guns firing above engine cowling; later-Serie aircraft also had two 7·7mm in wings; M.C.200 C.B. (caccia bombardiere) had underwing racks for two bombs of up to 352lb (160kg) each, or two 33gal drop tanks.
**History:** First flight 24 December 1937; service delivery October 1939; final delivery, about December 1944.
**User:** Italy.

**Development:** Mario Castoldi's design team at Aeronautica Macchi, at Varese in the north Italian lakeland, was the source of the best fighters used by the Regia Aeronautica in World War II. Castoldi's staff had earlier gained great experience with high-speed aircraft with their record-breaking Schneider seaplanes, but their first monoplane fighter, the C.200, bore little evidence of this. Though a reasonably attractive stressed-skin monoplane, it had an engine of low power and the performance was correspondingly modest. Moreover it never had anything that other countries would have regarded as proper armament, though the pilot did have the advantage of

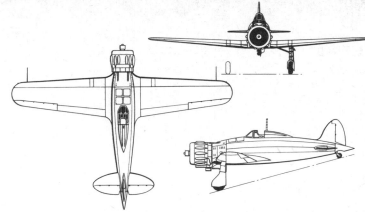

Above: Three-view of Macchi C.200 (late production serie).

cockpit indicators showing the number of rounds of ammunition unfired. Italian fighter pilots were by nature conservative; their protests caused the main production aircraft to have an open cockpit and fixed tailwheel, unlike the first batches, and combat equipment was simple in the extreme. Yet in combat with the lumbering Hurricane it proved effective, with outstanding dogfight performance and no vices. From late 1940 until Italy's surrender in September 1943 the C.200 saw more combat than any other Italian type, both around North Africa and Sicily and on the Eastern Front with the Corpo di Spedizone Italiano which claimed 88 Russian aircraft for the loss of 15 Saettas. The name Saetta, meaning lightning, refers to the lightning-bolts held by Jupiter, and is sometimes rendered as Arrow or Thunderbolt.

Left: A Macchi C.200 (or M.C.200 for Mario Castoldi) of a late serie in which the original sliding canopy had been replaced by a hinged hood open at the top. This one served the 90o Squadriglia, 10o Gruppo, 4o Stormo, based in Sicily in 1941.

Above: Takeoff of a section of Saettas of one of the late serie with wing guns but still an interim canopy.

Below: Contemporary colour photograph of Saettas parked amongst S.M.82 Canguru transports.

Above: An early-serie Saetta serving with the 81o Squadriglia, probably in 1940.

Below: A tactical base of the Regia Aeronautica, probably in southern Italy, with a Saetta and IMAM Meridionali Ro 37.

# Macchi C.202 and 205

## C.202 Folgore (Lightning), C.205V Veltro (Greyhound) and C.205N Orione (Orion)

**Origin:** Aeronautica Macchi; production also by SAI Ambrosini and Breda.
**Type:** Single-seat fighter (some, fighter bomber).
**Engine:** (202) 1,175hp Alfa Romeo RA1000 RC41-I (DB 601A-1) inverted-vee-12; (205) 1,475hp Fiat RA1050 RC58 Tifone (Typhoon) (DB 605A-1).
**Dimensions:** Span 34ft 8½in (10·58m) (205N, 36ft 11in, 11·25m); length 29ft 0½in (8·85m) (205N, 31ft 4in, 9·55m); height 9ft 11½in (3·04m) (205N, 10ft 8in, 3·25m).
**Weights:** Empty (202) 5,181lb (2350kg), (205V) 5,691lb (2581kg), (205N-2) 6,082lb (2759kg); loaded (202) 6,636lb (3010kg), (205V) 7,514lb (3408kg), (205N-2) 8,364lb (3794kg).
**Performance:** Maximum speed (202) 370mph (595km/h), (205V) 399mph (642km/h), (205N-2) 389mph (626km/h); service ceiling (all) about 36,000ft (11,000m).
**Armament:** See text.
**History:** First flight (202) 10 August 1940; service delivery (202) July 1941; final delivery, early 1944.
**User:** Italy (RA, CB, ARSI).

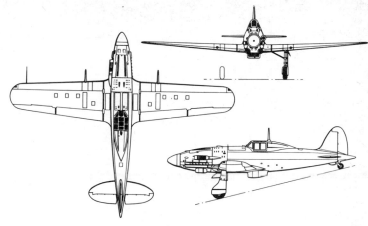

**Above:** Three-view of the Macchi C.205V Veltro.

**Below:** Wartime colour photograph of a Macchi C.202 Folgore taxiing out along a newly prepared taxiway. A ground-crewman rides on each wing, standard practice with poor-vision fighters.

**Left:** There were at least 25 authorised camouflage schemes used by Regia Aeronautica aircraft. This C.202 has one of the desert colour mixtures. Note the belly venturi.

**Right:** Another C.202 Folgore, fitted with the usual carburettor air-inlet sand filter. Note arms of the stormo and 73 Squadriglia.

**Left:** One of the C.205V Greyhounds to see active service. These aircraft were not outstanding in armament or performance, but beautiful to fly.

**Right:** Very few Macchi C.205N Oriones reached combat units. This example saw operational duty with the Aviazione Nazionale Repubblicana in December 1943.

**Above: An M.C.202 Serie III. These were among the best fighters of the war, though available only in trivial numbers.**

**Above: The prototype M.C.205V Veltro, first Italian fighter with the DB 605 engine, flown on 19 April 1942.**

▶**Development:** Essentially a re-engined Saetta, the MC202 was much more powerful and after quick and painless development went into production (first by Breda) in late 1940. Armament remained two 12·7mm Breda-SAFAT above the engine and two 7·7mm Breda-SAFAT in the wings, plus two bombs up to 353lb (160kg) or tanks. From the outset the cockpit was completely enclosed, opposition to this having finally withered. Up to Serie VIII many aircraft had no wing guns, while at least one Serie had two 20mm Mauser MG 151/20 in underwing fairings. About 1,500 were built by 1943, 392 by Macchi, achieving complete superiority over the Hurricane

and P-40. The more powerful 205 flew on 19 April 1942, but pathetic industrial performance (on engine as well as airframe) limited output to 262. The 205 Serie III dropped the 7·7mm wing guns in favour of MG 151/20s. The 205N was a total structural redesign instead of a converted 200, the first flying on 1 November 1942 with one MG 151/20 and four 12·7mm, two in the wing roots. It was an outstanding machine, retaining all the agility of earlier Macchi fighters, and the 205N-2 added powerful armament with two more MG 151/20 instead of the wing-root 12·7mm. None reached service.

**Left: Serving with the 11th Squadriglia, this C.202 Folgore is painted in one of the predominantly green camouflage schemes.**

**Right: Pinnacle of the Macchi single-engined fighter designs to reach the squadrons, the C.205N-1 combined superb handling with improved firepower. This one joined the Co-Belligerent Air Force.**

# Piaggio P.108

## P.108A, B, C, M and T

**Origin:** Società Anonima Piaggio & Cia.
**Type:** A, anti-shipping; B, bomber; C, civil; M, bomber; T, military transport.
**Engines:** Four 1,500hp Piaggio P.XII RC35 18-cylinder radials.

**Dimensions:** Span 104ft 11¾in (32·00m); length (B) 73ft 1½in (22·29m); height 19ft 8¼in (6·00m).
**Weights:** Empty (typical B) 36,375lb (16,500kg); max loaded 65,885lb (29,885kg).
**Performance:** Maximum speed (typical B) 267mph (430km/h); service ceiling 19,685ft (6000m); range with max bomb load 2,175 miles (3500km).
**Armament:** (B) eight 12·7mm Breda-SAFAT, two pairs in remote-sighted turrets above outer nacelles and four singles in nose and ventral turrets and waist positions; internal bay for three torpedoes or bomb load up to 7,716lb (3500kg).
**History:** First flight 1939; service delivery 1941; final delivery early 1944.
**Users:** Italy (RA, CB, ARSI), Germany (Luftwaffe).

**Development:** Derived from the P.50 of 1938, this large and powerful machine was the only Piaggio type to see much service in World War II, though 30 designs had been in use between the wars. The only model to see much use was the 108B (Bombardiere), of which 163 were built. Opening with night attacks on Gibraltar in early 1942, they later saw extensive service over North Africa, the Balkans, Soviet Union and Mediterranean (the Duce's son, Bruno Mussolini, was killed in one). The 16 C (Civile) aircraft were impressed as military transports, but the T (Trasporto) remained a prototype. The Luftwaffe took over the impressive 108A (Artiglieri) with 102mm gun in the forward fuselage. The M (Modificato) would have had a nose armament of one 20mm and four 7·7mm.

**Left: A regular P.108B in operational service with the Regia Aeronautica. Though it made little impact on the war, the big Piaggio was, in fact, one of the heaviest and most powerful bombers of the entire conflict.**

# Reggiane Re 2000 series

### Re 2000 Falco I (Falcon), 2001 Falco II, 2002 Ariete (Ram) and 2005 Sagittario (Archer)

**Origin:** Officine Meccaniche "Reggiane" SA; some Héjja built under licence by Mavag and Weiss Manfred, Hungary.
**Type:** Single-seat fighter.
**Engine:** (2000) one 1,025hp Piaggio P.XIbis RC40 14-cylinder two-row radial; (Héjja) 1,000hp WM K14; (2001) 1,175hp Alfa Romeo RA.1000 RC41 (DB 601) inverted-vee-12; (2002) 1,175hp Piaggio P.XIX RC45, (as P.XIbis); (2005) 1,475hp Fiat RA.1050 RC58 Tifone (Typhoon) (DB 605, as DB 601).
**Dimensions:** Span 36ft 1in (11m); length (2000) 26ft 2½in (7·95m); (2001–2) 26ft 10in; (2005) 28ft 7¾in; height (typical) 10ft 4in (3·15m).
**Weight:** Empty (2000) 4,200lb (1905kg); maximum loaded (2000) 5,722lb (2595kg); (2001) 7,231lb; (2002) 7,143lb; (2005) 7,848lb.
**Performance:** Maximum speed (2000–2) 329–337mph (say, 535km/h); (2005) 391mph (630km/h); initial climb (typical) 3,600ft (1100m)/min; service ceiling (2000) 36,745ft (11,200m); range (typical) 590 miles 950km).
**Armament:** See text.
**History:** First flight (2000) 1938; (2001) 1940; (2002) late 1941; (2005) September 1942.
**Users:** (Re 2000) Hungary, Italy (Navy), Sweden; (2001) Italy (RA and ARSI); (2002) Germany (Luftwaffe), Italy (ARSI); (2005) Germany (Luftwaffe), Italy (ARSI).

**Development:** A subsidiary of Caproni, the Reggiane company copied the Seversky P-35 to produce the nimble but lightly built Re 2000. Extremely manoeuvrable, it had two 12·7mm Breda-SAFAT on the top decking and could carry a 441lb (200kg) bomb. Almost all the 170 built served non-Italian forces, Sweden using 60 (as the J 20) and Hungary about 100 (as the Héjja) on the Eastern front. Production of the 2001 reached 252, in four series with two 12·7mm either alone or augmented by two 7·7mm or (in 150 CN2 night fighters) 20mm wing guns, plus a 1,410lb (640kg) bomb. About 50 2002 were built and only 48 of the excellent 2005 with three 20mm and two 12·7mm.

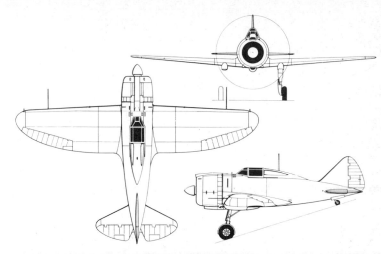

Above: Three-view of the Re 2000 Serie III.

Above: Very few radial-engined Reggiane fighters were delivered to the Regia Aeronautica. This appears to be an Re 2000-I.

Below: Almost certainly taken aboard the battleship Roma, this shows catapult trials of the Re 2000 Serie II.

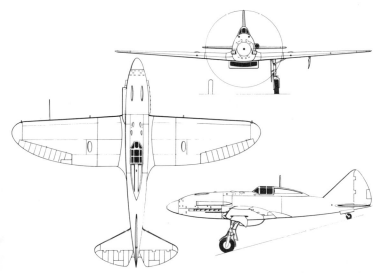

Above: Three-view of the Re 2005 Sagittario.

Below, right: Reggiane Re 2001 CN night fighters, serving with the Regia Aeronautica before the armistice of September 1943.

Below: MM 494, the first prototype Re 2005 Sagittario, flown in September 1942. Only about 48 were delivered.

Left: The Hungarian-built Héjja was an Re 2000 Serie Io with a Wright Cyclone R-1820 engine and many other changes. This example from 1/1 Fighter squadron was one of many which served on the Eastern Front.

V.4 ✛ 26

Right: Only one Regia Aeronautica unit, the 50˚ Stormo, was converting to the Re 2002 Ariete at the time of the armistice.

Left: An Re 2001 CN night fighter of the II° Gruppo Caccia, which after the armistice joined the Aviazione della RSI (the Aviazione Nazionale Repubblicana) under Luftwaffe direction, from October 1943.

Above: An Re 2001 CN of IIIa Series, armed with underwing 20mm cannon in addition to the two nose machine guns, in Regia Aeronautica service.

Top: Another night fighter, this time a Series IV° Re 2001 serving with the 82ª squadriglia, 21° Gruppo of the Italian Co-Belligerent Air Force.

**Reggiane Re 2001 Falco II cutaway drawing key**

1 Starboard navigation light
2 Starboard wingtip
3 Starboard aileron
4 Aileron control linkage
5 Corrugated inner wing skin
6 Flap structure
7 Starboard water radiator
8 Starboard 7.7-mm Breda-SAFAT machine gun
9 Ammunition tanks (600 rounds)
10 Gun muzzle
11 Blast tube
12 Engine cowling
13 Alfa-Romeo RA 1000 constant-speed propeller
14 Spinner
15 Propeller pitch change mechanism
16 Air inlet
17 Propeller mounting plate
18 Water system header tank
19 Alfa-Romeo RA 1000 RC 41-1a Monsonie 12-cylinder inverted-vee liquid-cooled engine
20 Anti-vibration engine mount
21 Forged aluminium engine bearer
22 Supercharger air intake
23 Intake filter
24 Supercharger
25 Ejector exhaust box
26 Oil cooler intake
27 Starboard mainwheel
28 Oil radiator
29 Oil radiator outlet flap
30 Coolant pipes
31 Oil tanks (6·38 Imp gal/29 l capacity)
32 Fuel filler cap
33 Engine bearer strut fixing
34 Ammunition tank (350 rpg)
35 Cartridge link ejector chute
36 Gun synchronisation mechanism
37 Port 12.7-mm Breda-SAFAT machine gun
38 Ammunition feed chutes
39 Cockpit front bulkhead
40 Instrument panel
41 Windscreen frame
42 Armourglass windscreen
43 S Giorgio Type B reflector sight
44 Standby bead-type sight
45 Machine gun breech housing
46 Canopy
47 Canopy top hinge
48 Canopy hinge (starboard side)
49 Sliding side windows
50 Headrest
51 Pilot's seat
52 Back-pack parachute housing
53 Fuselage upper box-section beam
54 Throttle and propeller central levers
55 Control condition
56 Rudder pedal
57 Fuselage lower box-section beam
58 Wing attachment angle beam
59 Flap and under-carriage gearbox
60 Emergency hand pump
61 Electric flap motor
62 Flap drive shaft
63 Bevel drive to flap linkage
64 Electric undercarriage motor
65 Fuselage fuel tank (17·6 Imp gal/80 l)
66 Tank filler pipe
67 Headrest support structure
68 Aerial mast
69 Aerial
70 Fuel filler cap
71 Rearward vision cut-out
72 Hydraulic reservoir access panel
73 Hydraulic reservoir
74 Modulator
75 Fuselage frames
76 Z-section stringers
77 Cockpit aft fairing
78 Fuselage upper skin plating
79 Pneumatic reservoir
80 CO₂ fire extinguisher bottle
81 Rudder cables
82 Elevator rod linkage
83 Fin fairing
84 Fin spar mounting
85 Starboard tailplane
86 Rudder trim linkage
87 Fin structure
88 Rudder post
89 Hinge box
90 Rudder structure
91 Aerial attachment
92 Rudder trim tab
93 Rear navigation light
94 Rudder operating arm
95 Port elevator
96 Elevator trim tab
97 Elevator control linkage
98 Tailplane structure
99 Tailwheel shock absorber
100 Castoring tailwheel
101 Tailplane attachment box-beam
102 Lifting point
103 Trim control cables
104 Fuselage lower skin plating
105 Batteries
106 Access hatch
107 TBR 30 radio transmitter and receiver
108 Wing root fillet
109 Port flap structure
110 Trailing edge structure
111 Aft wing fuel tank (44 Imp gal/200 l capacity)
112 Forward wing fuel tank (58 Imp gal/264 l capacity)
113 Wing upper skin (corrugated sandwich construction)
114 Port mainwheel well
115 Undercarriage drive shaft
116 Bevel gear housing
117 Undercarriage retraction screw jacks
118 Undercarriage 'pop-up' position indicator
119 Coolant pipes in leading edge
120 Undercarriage pivot mounting
121 Undercarriage leg fairing
122 Port gun muzzle
123 Main undercarriage leg
124 Shock absorber strut
125 Leg fairing door
126 Wheel cover plate
127 Port mainwheel
128 Pneumatic brake
129 Wing outer panel bolted joint
130 Port 7.7mm Breda-SAFAT machine-gun
131 Ammunition tanks (800 rounds)
132 Port wing radiator
133 Cooling air inlet
134 Radiator fairing
135 Cooling air outlet flap
136 Flap shroud construction
137 Multi-spar wing structure
138 Cranked rear spar
139 Intermediate spars
140 Front spar
141 Aileron control linkage
142 Port aileron
143 Aileron hinge mounting
144 Aileron trim tab
145 Lower wing skin
146 L-section stringers
147 Leading edge structure
148 Pitot head
149 Port navigation light
150 Wingtip construction

# Savoia-Marchetti S.M.79 Sparviero

## S.M.79-I, II and III, 79B and 79-JR

**Origin:** SIAI "Savoia-Marchetti"; built under licence (79-II) by Aeronautica Macchi and OM "Reggiane"; (79 JR) Industria Aeronautica Romana.
**Type:** 4/5-seat bomber, torpedo bomber and reconnaissance.
**Engines:** (I) three 780hp Alfa-Romeo 126 RC34 nine-cylinder radials; (II) three 1,000hp Piaggio P.XI RC40 14-cylinder two-row radials (one batch, 1,030hp Fiat A.80 RC41); (79B) two engines (many types); (79-JR) two 1,220hp Junker Jumo 211Da inverted-vee-12 liquid-cooled.
**Dimensions:** Span 69ft 6½in (21·2m); length (I) 51ft 10in; (II) 53ft 1¾in (16·2m); (B, -JR) 52ft 9in; height (II) 13ft 5½in (4·1m).

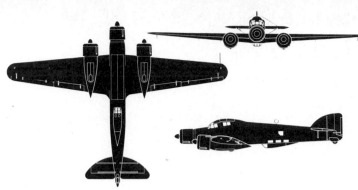

Above: Three-view of a typical S.M.79-II.

Left: A Savoia-Marchetti S.M.79-JR bomber of the 3rd Air Corps, Royal Air Forces of Romania, Eastern Front, 1943.

Below: S.M.79-II bombers of the Squadriglie Aerosiluranti (torpedo-bomber squadrons) with their weapons.

**Weights:** Empty (I) 14,990lb (6800kg); (II) 16,755lb (7600kg); (-JR) 15,860lb (7195kg); maximum loaded (I) 23,100lb (10,500kg); (II) 24,192lb (11,300kg); (-JR) 23,788lb (10,470kg).
**Performance:** Maximum speed (I) 267mph; (II) 270mph (434km/h); (B) 255mph; (-JR) 276mph; initial climb (typical) 1,150ft (350m)/min; service ceiling (all) 21,325–23,300ft (7000m); range with bomb load (not torpedoes), typical, 1,243 miles (2000km).
**Armament:** (Typical) one 12·7mm Breda-SAFAT fixed firing ahead from above cockpit, one 12·7mm manually aimed from open dorsal position, one 12·7mm manually aimed from rear of ventral gondola and one 7·7mm Lewis manually aimed from either beam window; internal bomb bay for up to 2,200lb (1000kg) or two 450mm torpedoes slung externally; (79B and -JR) no fixed gun, typically three/five 7·7mm guns and bomb load up to 2,640lb (1200kg).
**History:** First flight (civil prototype) late 1934; service delivery (I) late 1936; (II) October 1939; final delivery (III) early 1944.
**Users:** Brazil, Iraq, Italy (RA, CB, ARSI), Jugoslavia, Romania, Spain (Nationalist).

**Development:** Though often derided — as were most Italian arms in World War II — the S.M.79 Sparviero (Hawk) was a fine and robust bomber that unfailingly operated in the most difficult conditions with great reliability. The prototype, fitted with various engines and painted in civil or military liveries, set various world records in 1935–36, despite its mixed structure of steel tube, light alloy, wood and fabric. Built at unprecedented rate for the Regia Aeronautica, the 79-I established an excellent·reputation with

the Aviación Legionaria in the Spanish civil war, while other Stormi laid the basis for great proficiency with torpedoes. Altogether about 1,200 of all versions served with the Regia Aeronautica, while just over 100 were exported. Most exports were twin-engined 79B versions, but the Romanian-built 79-JR was more powerful and served on the Russian front in 1941–44.

Below: Early S.M.79-I bombers of the Regia Aeronautica's 52o Squadriglia, photographed just before the war.

22

# Savoia-Marchetti S.M.81 Pipistrello

## S.M.81 Pipistrello (Bat) of many serie

**Origin:** SIAI "Savoia-Marchetti".
**Type:** Multi-role bomber, transport and utility.
**Engines:** (Most) three aircooled radials, usually 700hp Piaggio P.X nine-cylinder; others 580hp Alfa Romeo 125, 680hp Piaggio P.IX, 900hp Alfa Romeo 126 and 1,000hp Gnome-Rhône K-14; (81B, two engines, various).
**Dimensions:** Span 78ft 8¾in (24·00m); length (typical) 58ft 4¾in (17·80 m); height 14ft 7¼in (4·45m).
**Weights:** Empty (typical) 13,890lb (6300kg); max loaded 23,040lb (10,450kg).
**Performance:** Maximum speed 211mph (340km/h); typical range with bomb load 932 miles (1500km).

**Below:** Before Italy joined World War II many S.M.81 bombers had brightly painted upper surfaces (for forced landings).

**Above:** A pair of Pipistrello bombers, in silver or cream dope overall, on maritime reconnaissance duty. Note the large ventral gondola for the bomb aimer, a feature of several Italian aircraft.

**Armament:** Varied or absent, but usually two 7·7mm Breda-SAFAT in powered dorsal turret, two more in retractable ventral turret and two more aimed manually from beam windows; internal weapon bay for up to 2,205lb (1000kg) of bombs.
**History:** First flight 1935; service delivery, autumn 1935; final delivery, possibly 1941.
**Users:** Italy (RA, CB, ARSI, post-war AF), Spain.

**Development:** A military version of the very successful S.M.73 airliner, the S.M.81 was one of the world's best multi-role bomber/transport aircraft in 1935, but when Italy entered World War II in June 1940 (by which time about 100 were in service, plus about 40 in Spain) it was becoming obsolescent. Despite this its serviceability and popularity resulted in it appearing in every theatre in which Italy was engaged, from Eritrea to the Soviet Union. Until 1942 it was an important night bomber in the eastern Mediterranean, and it became the most important Italian transport in terms of numbers (though much inferior to the S.M.82 in capability). A few served with the post-war Aeronautica Militare until about 1951.

# Savoia-Marchetti S.M.82 Canguru

## S.M.82 Canguru (Kangaroo) of various serie

**Origin:** SIAI "Savoia-Marchetti".
**Type:** Heavy freight and troop transport.
**Engines:** Three 950hp Alfa Romeo 128RC21 nine-cylinder radials.
**Dimensions:** Span 96ft 9½in (29·50m); length 73ft 9¾in (22·50m); height 18ft 0½in (5·50m).
**Weights:** Empty 26,455lb (12,000kg); loaded 39,728lb (18,020kg).
**Performance:** Maximum speed 204mph (328km/h); range with unspecified payload at 137mph (220km/h) 2,467 miles (3970km).
**Armament:** Usually Breda-SAFAT retractable hydraulic turret with one or two 12·7mm, plus two to five 7·7mm manually aimed from side windows; large internal bomb bay seldom used except for overload fuel tanks.
**History:** First flight 1939; final delivery 1943.
**Users:** Germany (Luftwaffe), Italy (RA, CB, ARSI, post-war AF), UK (RAF), US (AAF).

**Development:** An enlarged development of the S.M.75 Marsupiale, the Canguru was the most capable transport in large-scale service with the Axis during most of the war, and because of its unique capability was used

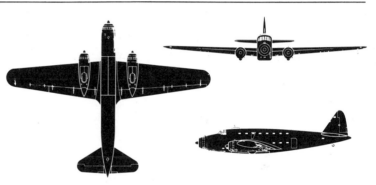

**Above: Three-view of S.M.82 Canguru.**

in substantial numbers even by the Luftwaffe. Though clearly underpowered, so that even with all three engines the rate of climb was pathetic (and near-zero at the seldom-used max overload weight of 20,000kg, 44,092lb), the Canguru was reliable and fully equipped with handling gear for aero engines and even dismantled fighters. Folding seats for 40 troops were provided (96 were once carried), and a normal fuel load was 15 to 18 drums of 40 Imp gal. The wing was wood, like most S.M. products, and the cavernous body steel tube and fabric. In September 1943 no fewer than 31 of these giants flew to join the Allies, and five were still in RAF foreign service in 1947.

**Below:** A Canguru loading torpedoes, without warheads. On the extreme right is an extremely rare bird, a Breda Ba 88 Lince (Lynx) twin-engined attack aircraft.

**Below: The pot-bellied Canguru looked ungainly, and it was certainly underpowered, but it was probably the most capable transport in the whole armoury of the Axis powers.**

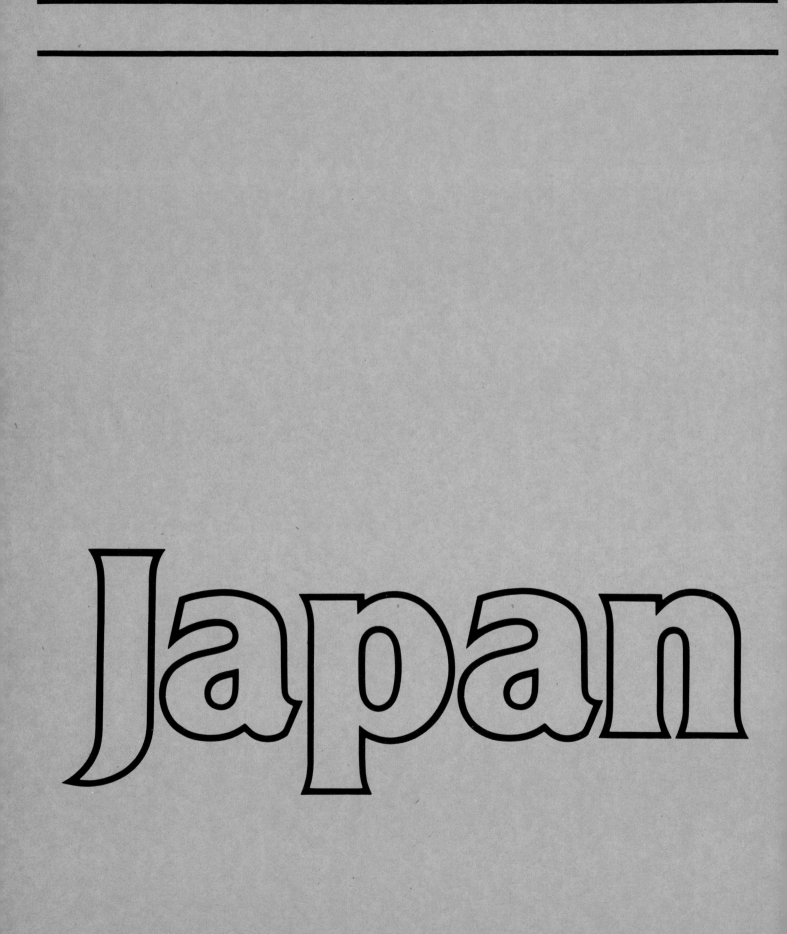

# Aichi D3A "Val"

## D3A1 and D3A2

**Origin:** Aichi Tokei Denki KK.
**Type:** Two-seat carrier dive bomber.
**Engine:** 1,075hp Mitsubishi Kinsei 44 14-cylinder radial (D3A2, 1,200hp Kinsei 54).
**Dimensions:** Span 47ft 1½in (14·365m); (D3A2) 47ft 8in (14·53m); length 33ft 5½in (10·2m); (D3A2) 33ft 7in (10·25m); height 11ft (3·35m); (D3A2 same).
**Weights:** Empty 5,309lb (2408kg); (D3A2) 5,772lb (2618kg); loaded 8,047lb (3650kg); (D3A2) 8,378lb (3800kg).
**Performance:** Maximum speed 242mph (389km/h); (D3A2) 281mph (450km/h); service ceiling 31,170ft (9500m); (D3A2) 35,700ft (10,880m); range with bomb 1,131 miles (1820km); (D3A2) 969 miles (1560km).
**Armament:** Two fixed 7·7mm guns in wings, one pivoted in rear cockpit; centreline bomb of 551lb (250kg), plus two bombs under wings each of 66lb (30kg); (D3A2; wing bombs 132lb, 60kg).
**History:** First flight August 1936; (D3A2) probably 1941; termination of production 1944.
**User:** Imperial Japanese Navy.

**Development:** In World War II the proper designations of Japanese aircraft were difficult to remember and often unknown to the Allies, so each major type was allotted a codename. Even today "Aichi D3A" may mean little to a grizzled veteran to whom the name "Val" will evoke memories of terrifying dive-bombing attacks. Aichi began this design for the Imperial Navy in 1936, its shape showing the influence of Heinkel who were secretly advising the Navy at that time. A total of 478 D3A1, also called Model 11 or Type 99, were built by August 1942, when production switched to the D3A2, Model 22. The D3A1 was the dive bomber that attacked Pearl Harbor on 7 December 1941. In April 1942 Aichis confirmed their bomb-hitting accuracy of 80–82% by sinking the British carrier *Hermes* and heavy cruisers *Cornwall* and *Dorsetshire*. They were extremely strong and manoeuvrable, and until 1943 were effective dogfighters after releasing their bombs. But loss of skilled pilots in great battles of 1943–44, especially Midway and the Solomons, reduced bombing accuracy to 10% and the Aichis ceased to be the great threat they were in 1942. Production of the D3A2 was stopped in January 1944 at the 816th example of this cleaner and better-looking version. Some Aichis were converted as trainers or as overloaded Kamikaze aircraft. Nakajima developed a smaller version with retractable landing gear, the D3N1, but this was not adopted.

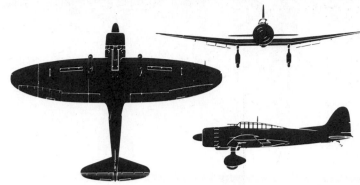

**Above:** Three-view of the cleaned-up Aichi D3A2.

**Above:** Takeoff of a D3A1 from a Japanese carrier on 7 December 1941, en route for Pearl Harbor and World War II.

**Right:** The Aichi D3A1 was one of the world's best dive bombers at the time of its design in 1935. Also called Navy Dive Bomber Type 99 Model 11, it equipped Japanese carriers until the end of 1942.

**Below:** The later Val, the D3A2, or Type 99 Model 22, was a still better aircraft but never enjoyed Japanese air supremacy.

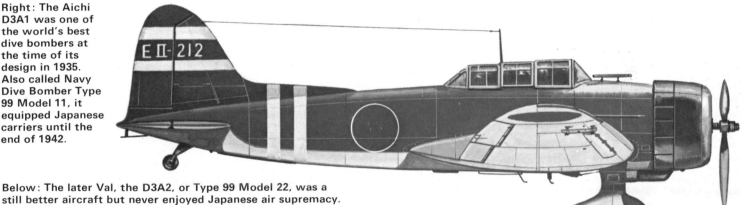

# Aichi B7A Ryusei "Grace"

**AM-23, 16-Shi Carrier Attack Bomber Ryusei (Shooting Star) (Allied code-name "Grace")**

**Origin:** Aichi Kokuki KK; second-source production by Dai-Nijuichi Kaigun Kokusho (Sasebo Naval Air Arsenal).
**Type:** Two-seat carrier-based torpedo and dive bomber.
**Engine:** 1,825hp Nakajima NK9C Homare 12 18-cylinder radial.
**Dimensions:** Span 47ft 3in (14·40m); length 37ft 8½in (11·49m); height 13ft 4¼in (4·07m).
**Weights:** Empty 7,969lb (3614kg); loaded 12,568lb (5700kg).
**Performance:** Maximum speed 352mph (566km/h); service ceiling 29,365ft (8950m); range with full weapon load 1,150 miles (1850km); max range (overload) 1,889 miles (3040km).
**Armament:** Two 20mm Type 99 Model 2 in wings and single 7·92mm or 13mm gun aimed from rear cockpit; one 1,764lb (800kg) torpedo or similar weight of bombs.
**History:** First flight May 1942; service delivery May 1944; final delivery August 1945.
**User:** Japan (Imperial Navy).

**Development:** One of Japan's largest and most powerful carrier-based aircraft, the B7A was designed to a 1941 (16-Shi) specification for a fast and versatile aircraft to supplement and then replace the Nakajima B6N torpedo bomber and Yokosuka D4Y dive bomber. Though it did not carry

**Above:** A rare photograph of a fully operational B7A, complete with torpedo, apparently about to depart on a combat mission. Every operational flight was from land airstrips.

any more weapons than its predecessors, the B7A1 prototype proved to be greatly superior in performance, with speed and manoeuvrability at least as good as an A6M "Zero". Unfortunately the troublesome engine delayed development until Japan had lost command of the air, and by the time deliveries took place the last carriers were being sunk and home industry bombed to a standstill (the destruction of the Aichi Funakata plant by a May 1945 earthquake did not help). Only 114 aircraft flew, nine being B7A1 prototypes and the rest B7A2 production machines used from land bases.

---

# Aichi E16A Zuiun "Paul"

**AM-22, E16A1 Zuiun (Auspicious Cloud) (Allied code-name "Paul")**

**Origin:** Aichi Kokuki KK; production transferred in 1944 to Nippon Hikoki KK.
**Type:** Two-seat reconnaissance seaplane.
**Engine-** 1,300hp Mitsubishi Kinsei 51 or 54 14-cylinder radial.
**Dimensions:** Span 42ft 0¼in (12·80m); length 35ft 6½in (10·84m); height 15ft 8½in (4·74m).
**Weights:** Empty 5,982lb (2713kg); loaded 8,379lb (3800kg); max overload 9,327lb (4230kg).
**Performance:** Maximum speed 278mph (448km/h); service ceiling 33,730ft (10,280m); range (normal) 600 miles (965km), (overload) 1,578 miles (2540km).
**Armament:** Two 20mm Type 99 cannon in wings and one 13mm Type 2 aimed from rear cockpit; one or two 551lb (250kg) bombs or other stores.
**History:** First flight May 1942; service delivery January 1944; final delivery August 1945.
**User:** Japan (Imperial Navy).

**Development:** This aircraft was designed to a 16-Shi (1941) specification for a much faster replacement for the E13A1, even though the latter was not then in service. The E16A1 had hydraulic dive brakes forming the fairings of the front float struts and could undertake steep diving attacks. Nevertheless, it was not as popular as its predecessor, and as the Allies enjoyed complete air superiority by 1944 it suffered heavily and seldom worked

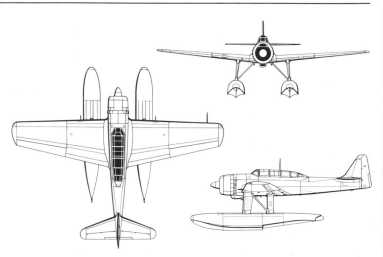

**Above: Three-view of E16A1 Zuiun.**

unhindered. Total production was only 256, Nippon Hikoki having mainly unskilled-student labour and being under heavy air attack. A single E16A2 flew with a 1,560hp Kinsei 62 engine.

**Below: An excellent photograph of a production E16A1, which emphasizes the drag and weight penalty of the large float landing gear. Most crews preferred the old E13A1.**

# Aichi E13A "Jake"

## E13A1, Navy Type 0 Reconnaissance Seaplane Model 11 (Allied code-name "Jake").

**Origin:** Aichi Tokei Denki KK; production also by Dai-Juichi Kaigun Kokusho (Hiro Naval Air Arsenal) and Kyushu Hikoki KK (Watanabe).
**Type:** Three-seat reconnaissance seaplane.
**Engine:** 1,080hp Mitsubishi Kinsei 43 14-cylinder radial.
**Dimensions:** Span 47ft 6¾in (14·50m); length 36ft 11¾in (11·27m); height 15ft 8in (4·79m).
**Weights:** Empty 5,825lb (2642kg); max loaded 8,048lb (3650kg).
**Performance:** Maximum speed 239mph (385km/h); service ceiling 26,100ft (7950m); maximum range 1,616 miles (2600km).
**Armament:** One 7·92mm Type 1 machine gun (based on German MG 15) aimed from rear cockpit, most late production in addition one 20mm Type 99 added as field modification firing down in limited arc from belly; four 132lb (60kg) bombs or depth charges — rarely, one 551lb (250kg).
**History:** First flight late 1938; service delivery 1941; final delivery August 1945.
**User:** Japan (Imperial Navy).

**Development:** Though never famous, the E13A1 was made in larger numbers than any other Japanese floatplane, or marine aircraft of any type, and served on all fronts. Designed to a 1937 specification for a replacement for the Kawanishi E7K2, it was selected over rival aircraft from Kawanishi and Nakajima despite being larger and heavier. After various delays and changes Aichi got into production in December 1940. Operating from cruiser catapults and from seaplane tenders it made its debut in China in attacks on the Canton-Hangkow railway, and later reconnoitred Pearl Harbor before the attack of 7 December 1941. Despite poor armament this seaplane served in many roles including air/sea rescue and, in late 1944, Kamikaze attacks. By this time examples were being equipped with a cannon for strafing ships, improved radio and primitive MAD (magnetic anomaly detection) gear for finding submerged submarines. Production totalled 1,418.

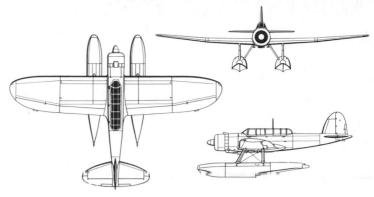

**Above:** Three-view of E13A1, without ventral cannon.

**Below:** A late-production E13A1 on its beaching chassis. Like the British Swordfish, it was more popular than its replacement.

# Kawanishi H6K "Mavis"

## H6K1 to H6K5, Navy Type 97 Large Flying Boat Models 1, 11, 22 and 23 (Allied code-name "Mavis")

**Origin:** Kawanishi Kokuki KK, Naruo.
**Type:** Long-range reconnaissance flying boat with crew of nine; (H6K3, H6K2-L and H6K4-L) transport.
**Engines:** Four Mitsubishi Kinsei 14-cylinder radials, (most) 1,000hp Kinsei 43, (H6K4 and 4-L) 1,070hp Kinsei 46, (H6K5) 1,300hp Kinsei 51 or 53.
**Dimensions:** Span 131ft 2¾in (40·00m); length 84ft 1in (25·63m); height 20ft 6¾in (6·27m).
**Weights:** Empty (H6K2) 22,796lb (10,340kg), (H6K5) 27,293lb (12,380 kg); normal loaded (1) 35,274lb (16,000kg), (5) 38,581lb (17,500kg); max loaded (1) as normal, (5) 50,706lb (23,000kg).
**Performance:** Maximum speed (1-4 typical) 207mph (333km/h), (5) 239mph (385km/h); range (most, normal) 2,690 miles (4330km), (5, normal) 3,107 miles (5000km), (5, max) 4,210 miles (6775km).
**Armament:** (1, 2, typical) hand-aimed 7·7mm Type 92 machine guns in bow and stern, plus a third in dorsal turret, (4, 5) 20mm Type 99 in tail turret and four or five 7·7mm Type 92 in nose, dorsal and beam blisters; (1, 2, 4, 5) two 1,764lb (800kg) torpedoes or total 2,205lb (1000kg) of bombs; (transport versions) no armament.

**History:** First flight 14 July 1936; service delivery January 1938; final delivery, mid-1943.
**User:** Japan (Imperial Navy).

**Development:** Obviously inspired by the Sikorsky S-42 but having a markedly superior performance, the H6K was an excellent machine and with an endurance of 26 hours made numerous outstanding missions. Until mid-1942 it was often engaged in bombing and torpedo attack, but lack of armour and self-sealing tanks caused even the H6K5 soon to revert to various auxiliary and (suffix L) transport roles. Altogether 215 of these graceful machines were delivered, the 2-L and 4 L transports normally seating up to 18 passengers and serving as the chief long-range Navy transports in the vast area held by the Japanese in the south-west Pacific. Several operated to airline-type schedules.

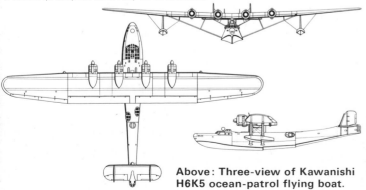

**Above:** Three-view of Kawanishi H6K5 ocean-patrol flying boat.

**Right:** One of a classic air-combat photographic sequence showing an H6K5 being shot down by Allied aircraft over the south-west Pacific. They usually flew alone.

# Kawanishi H8K "Emily"

## H8K1, H8K2; Type 2

**Origin:** Kawanishi Kokuki KK.
**Type:** Reconnaissance and attack flying boat.
**Engines:** Four Mitsubishi Kasei 14-cylinder two-row radials, (H8K1, Model 11) 1,530hp Kasei 12; (H8K2, Model 12) 1,850hp Kasei 22.
**Dimensions:** Span 124ft 8in (38m); length 92ft 3½in (28·1m); height 30ft 0¼in (9·15m).
**Weights:** Empty (H8K1) 34,000lb (15,440kg); (H8K2) 40,500lb (18,380 kg); loaded (H8K1) 68,343lb (31,000kg); (H8K2) 71,650lb (32,500kg).
**Performance:** Maximum speed (H8K1) 270mph (433km/h); (H8K2) 282mph (454km/h); initial climb 1,575ft (480m)/min; service ceiling 28,800ft (8770m); range, usually 3,000 miles (4800km), but overload reconnaissance range 4,474 miles (7200km).
**Armament:** Normally, five 20mm in power-driven nose, dorsal and tail

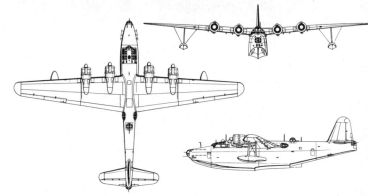

**Above: Three-view of Kawanishi H8K2.**

# Kawanishi N1K1-J and 2-J Shiden "George"

## N1K1-J and N1K2-J and variants

**Origin:** Kawanishi Kokuki KK; also built by Omura Kaigun Kokusho, Mitsubishi, Aichi, Showa and Dai-Juichi.
**Type:** Single-seat fighter.
**Engine:** One 1,990hp Nakajima Homare 21 18-cylinder two-row radial.
**Dimensions:** Span 39ft 3¼in (11·97m); length 29ft 1¾in (8·885m); (N1K2-J) 30ft 8¼in (9·35m); height 13ft 3¾in (4·058m); (N1K2-J) 13ft (3·96m).
**Weights:** Empty 6,387lb (2897kg); (N1K2-J) 6,299lb (2657kg); maximum loaded 9,526lb (4321kg); (N1K2-J) 10,714lb (4860kg).
**Performance:** Maximum speed 362mph (583km/h); (N1K2-J) 369mph (594km/h); initial climb (both) 3,300ft (1000m)/min; service ceiling 39,698ft (12,100m); (N1K2-J) 35,400ft (10,760m); range 989 miles (1430km); (N1K2-J) 1,069 miles (1720km).
**Armament:** Originally two 20mm in wings and two 7·7mm above fuselage; after 20 aircraft, two extra 20mm added in underwing blisters; (N1K1-Ja) as before without 7·7mm; N1K2-J, four 20mm in pairs inside wing, with more ammunition, plus two 550lb (250kg) bombs underwing or six rockets under fuselage; later prototypes, heavier armament.
**History:** First flight 24 July 1943; first flight (N1K2-J) 3 April 1944.
**User:** Japan (Imperial Navy).

**Development:** In September 1940 the JNAF issued a requirement for a high-speed seaplane naval fighter that did not need land airfields but could maintain air superiority during island invasions. The result was the formidable N1K1 Kyofu (mighty wind), produced by Kawanishi's Naruo plant and code-named "Rex" by the Allies. It was from this central-float seaplane that Kikuhara's team very quickly devised the N1K1-J landplane (Allied name: "George"). Though a hasty lash-up it was potentially one of

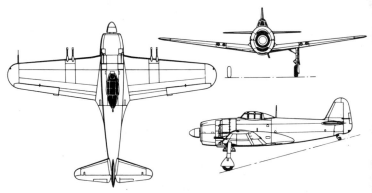

**Above: Three-view of N1K2-J Shiden-Kai.**

the best of all Japanese fighters. Its manoeuvrability, boosted by automatic combat flaps worked by a manometer (mercury U-tube) that measured angle of attack, was almost unbelievable. Drawbacks were the engine, plagued with snags, the poor view with the mid wing and the complex and weak landing gear (legacy from the mid-wing float-plane and big four-blade propeller). Naruo therefore produced the N1K2-J with low wing, new tail and drastically simpler airframe that could be built in half the man-hours. The unreliable engine still kept Shidens (the name meant violet lightning) mostly unserviceable, but they were potent and respected adversaries, encountered on all fronts from May 1944. Total production was 1,440. Huge production was planned from four companies and four Navy arsenals, but none produced more than ten aircraft, other than Kawanishi which delivered 543 1-Js and 362 2-Js from Naruo and 468 1-Js and 44 2-Js from Himeji. At Okinawa both versions were used in the Kamikaze role.

**Right: Built from 23,000 fewer parts than the original mass-produced Shiden, the N1K2-J was an outstanding fighter in all respects, but appeared too late and in too-few numbers.**

**Above:** A dramatic combat photograph taken, like that above right, from a USAAF B-26 Marauder. The latter's heavy armament defeated the cannon carried by the big flying boat.

**Above:** In this picture the "Emily", an H8K2, is going gently down towards the Pacific, whilst starting to burn. Even Allied fighter pilots treated this boat with respect, because most had an armament including five 20mm cannon.

**Left:** An H8K2 assigned to the Imperial Japanese Navy's Yokohama Air Corps. It was an outstanding aircraft.

**Left:** An air-combat photograph of exceptional clarity for its time (1944). The H8K2 was the most powerful and most formidable long-range ocean patrol aircraft used by any of the combatants in World War II.

turrets and three 7·7mm manually aimed from beam and ventral rear windows; weapon load slung beneath inner wing, comprising two torpedoes or bombs to total weight of 4,410lb (2000kg); (H8K2-L) one 20mm and one 12·7mm, both manually aimed.

**History:** First flight late 1940; (production H8K1) August 1941.

**User:** Japan (Imperial Navy).

**Development:** Throughout the early part of the Pacific War the standard ocean patrol flying boat of the Imperial Japanese Navy was the Kawanishi H6K family (known to the Allies as "Mavis"). Though Kawanishi had a technical agreement with Short Brothers, the H6K looked like a Sikorsky S.42. It was an excellent aircraft, 217 being delivered including 36 transport versions. The question of a replacement was a challenge and the JNAF published a specification in 1938 calling for 30 per cent higher speed and 50 per cent greater range. In the H8K, Kawanishi's design team, under Dr Kikuhara, created a flying boat which has served as the biggest single jump in the technology of such aircraft in all history. It was beyond dispute the best and most advanced flying boat in the world until many years after World War II. Its early trials were disastrous, because the great weight and narrow-beamed hull resulted in uncontrollable porpoising. The cure was found in adding a second step in the planing bottom, adjusting the powerful double-slotted Fowler flaps and adding a horizon mark on the large pitot post above the bows. Altogether the Kohnan plant built 17 H8K1, 114 H8K2 and 36 of the H8K2-L transport version (Allied name: "Emily"). They ranged alone on daring 24-hour missions and proved formidable. Their first sortie, in March 1942, was to have been a bombing raid on Oahu, Hawaii, with an intermediate refuelling from a submarine, but the target lay under dense low cloud. Later H8K2 versions carried radar and two had retractable stabilizing floats.

# Kawasaki Ki-45 Toryu "Nick"

## Ki-45 and 45A, Heavy Fighter Type 2, Kai B, C and D

**Origin:** Kawasaki Kokuki Kogyo.
**Type:** Originally long-range escort; later night fighter and attack.
**Engines:** Two 1,080hp Mitsubishi Ha-102 (Type 1) 14-cylinder two-row radials.
**Dimensions:** Span 49ft 3½in (15·02m); length (Kai C) 36ft 1in (11m); height 12ft 1½in (3·7m).
**Weights:** Empty (Kai A) 8,340lb (3790kg); (Kai C) 8,820lb (4000kg); loaded (all) 12,125lb (5500kg).
**Performance:** Maximum speed (all) 336mph (540km/h); initial climb 2,300ft (700m)/min; service ceiling 32,800ft (10,000m); range, widely conflicting reports, but best Japanese sources suggest 1,243 miles (2000km) with combat load for all versions.
**Armament:** (Ki-45-I and Kai-A) two 12·7mm fixed in nose and two 7·7 mm manually aimed from rear cockpit; (Kai-B) same plus 37mm cannon in lower right forward fuselage (often with only one 12·7mm); (Kai-C) adapted for night fighting in May 1944, two 12·7mm installed at 30° between cockpits, with two 12·7mm and one 20mm or 37mm in nose; antiship versions, said to have carried 50mm or 75mm gun under nose, plus two 551lb (250kg) bombs under wings.
**History:** First flight (Ha-20 engine) January 1939; (Ha-25 engine) July 1940; (production Ki-45) September 1941.
**User:** Japan (Imperial Army).

**Development:** The first twin-engined fighter of the Imperial Japanese Army, the Ki-45 Toryu (dragon-slayer) was a long time in gestation. It was designed at Kawasaki's Gifu factory to meet a 1936 requirement issued in March 1937. Kawasaki had never used twin air-cooled engines and the Nakajima Ha-20B was an undeveloped engine which misbehaved; pilots disliked the hand-cranked landing gear. After trying contraprops, the choice fell on the Navy Ha-25 Sakae engine, but this in turn was replaced by the Ha-102 soon after production began in 1941. The Akashi plant began to

**Above: Three-view of Kawasaki Ki-45 Kai-B with 37mm cannon; the Kai-C night fighter added two oblique upward-firing guns.**

build the Ki-45 as a second source in late 1942, but combined output was only 1,698. Despite this modest total, and the fact that these aircraft were continually being modified, they were met on every Pacific front and known as "Nick". They were fairly fast and manoeuvrable but not really formidable until, on 27 May 1944, four Kai-B (modification B) made the first-ever suicide attack (on the north coast of New Guinea). By mid-1944 most Ki-45s had been modified to Kai-C configuration as night fighters, claiming seven victories over B-29s on the night of 15 June 1944. The two main Ki-45 bases at the close of the war were Hanoi and Anshan (Manchuria), from which aircraft made night interceptions and day Kamikaze attacks. The Ki-45 never operated in its design role of long-range escort.

**Right: An early Ki-45, probably used as an engineering test aircraft since it does not bear the badge of a fighter training school. Engines are Ha-25s.**

**Left: One of the most colourful late-war examples was this Ki-45-Hei (Kai-C) based at Matsudo, Chiba Prefecture, in August 1945. It belongs to the 53rd Sentai (note badge on tail) and was assigned to the Shinten unit (anti-B-29).**

# Kawasaki Ki-48 "Lily"

## Ki-48-I, -IIa, -IIb and -IIc (Allied code-name "Lily")

**Origin:** Kawasaki Kokuki Kogyo KK.
**Type:** Four-seat light bomber.
**Engines:** Two 14-cylinder radials, (-I) 980hp Nakajima Ha-25 (Army Type 99), (-II) 1,150hp Nakajima Ha-115 (Army Type 1).
**Dimensions:** Span 57ft 3¾in (17·47m); length (-I) 41ft 4in (12·60m), (-II) 41ft 10in (12·75m); height 12ft 5½in (3·80m).
**Weights:** Empty (-I) 8,928lb (4050kg), (-II) 10,030lb (4550kg); loaded (-I) 13,337lb (6050kg), (-II) 14,880lb (6750kg).
**Performance:** Maximum speed (-I) 298mph (480km/h), (-II) 314mph (505km/h); range (both, bomb load not specified) 1,491 miles (2400km).
**Armament:** (most) three 7·7mm Type 89 manually aimed from nose, dorsal and ventral positions, (-IIc) two Type 89 in nose, one ventral and manually aimed 12·7mm Type 1 dorsal; (all) internal bay for bomb load of

**Above: The Ki-48-IIb was fitted with snow-fence type dive-bombing airbrakes above and below the wings.**

up to 882lb (400kg), with normal load of 661lb (300kg) (-II capable of carrying 1,764lb, 800kg, but seldom used).
**History:** First flight July 1939; service delivery July or August 1940; final delivery October 1944.
**User:** Japan (Imperial Army).

**Development:** The Imperial Army's procurement organization tended to plan aircraft to meet existing, rather than future, threats. This straightforward bomber was requested in answer to the Soviet Union's SB-2. The latter was designed in 1933 and in action in Spain in 1936, but the Ki-48 (which was inferior in bomb load and only slightly faster) was a World War II machine. Entering service in China, it did well and proved popular, and it soon became the most important light bomber in the south-west Pacific with 557 -I built by June 1942. But its deficient performance and protection forced it to operate by night, which reduced the effectiveness of the small bomb load. The lengthened and more powerful -IIa had armour and protected tanks, and the -IIb had dive-bombing airbrakes; later examples of both had a dorsal fin. The -IIc had better armament, with provision also for machine guns fired from each side of the nose, but the Ki-48 was inherently obsolete and after a total of 1,977 of all versions production stopped in 1944. Many were used for suicide attacks and as test-beds for missiles and the Ne-00 turbojet (carried on a pylon under the bomb bay).

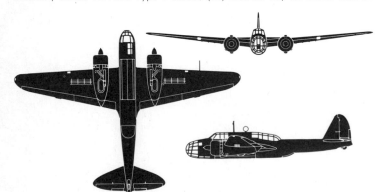

**Above: Three-view of Ki-48-IIb (IIc similar).**

# Kawasaki Ki-102 "Randy"

## Ki-102a, b and c
## (Allied code-name "Randy")

**Origin:** Kawasaki Kokuki Kogyo KK.
**Type:** Two-seat (a) high-altitude fighter, (b) ground-attack aircraft or (c) night fighter.
**Engines:** Two 1,500hp Mitsubishi Ha-112 14-cylinder radials, (a, c) Ha-112-II Ru with turbochargers.
**Dimensions:** Span (a, b) 51ft 1in (15·57m), (c) 56ft 6¼in (17·23m); length (a, b) 37ft 6¾in (11·45m), (c) 42ft 9¾in (13·05m); height 12ft 1¾in (3·70m).
**Weights:** Empty (a) 11,354lb (5150kg), (b) 10,913lb (4950kg), (c) 11,464lb (5200kg); loaded (a) 15,763lb (7150kg), (b) 16,094lb (7300kg), (c) 16,755lb (7600kg).
**Performance:** Maximum speed (a, b) 360mph (580km/h), (c) 373mph (600km/h); service ceiling (a) 42,650ft (13,000m), (b) 32,800ft (10,000m),

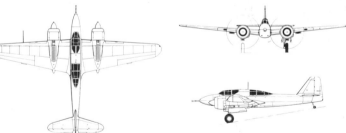

Above: Ki-102b with long-barrel 57mm and without D/F acorn.

(c) 44,295ft (13,500m); range (a, b) 1,243 miles (2000km), (c) 1,367 miles (2200km).
**Armament:** (a) one fixed 37mm Ho-203 in nose and two 20mm Ho-5 below, (b) one 57mm Ho-401 in nose, two Ho-5 below and manually aimed 12·7mm Ho-103 in rear cockpit, (c) two 30mm Ho-105 under fuselage and two 20mm Ho-5 mounted obliquely.
**History:** First flight March 1944; service delivery, about November 1944.
**User:** Japan (Imperial Army).

**Below:** A standard Ki-102b after capture. This has the D/F loop acorn above the fuselage and the short-barrel 57mm gun.

**Development:** In August 1942 the Ki-45 Toryu design team under Takeo Doi began work on a development designated Ki-96, three of these 3,000hp single-seat "heavy fighters" being built. In August 1943 approval was given for a further development with crew of two for use in the ground-attack role. Three prototypes and 20 pre-production Ki-102 were built, followed by 215 Ki-102b (Ki-102 Otsu) of which a few saw action in Okinawa. Some were used in the Igo-1-B air-to-ground missile programme. Two were rebuilt with pressure cabin as prototypes of the Ki-108, but the size of development task for this led to the Ki-102a being launched as a high-altitude fighter without pressure cabin. About 15 were delivered in July-August 1945 as the Ki-102 Ko. Right at the end of the war two Ki-102b were completely rebuilt as prototypes of the 102c night fighter with AI radar, greater span and length, new cockpit with rear-facing radar operator and different armament.

# Kawasaki Ki-61 Hien "Tony"

## Ki-61-I, II and III (Type 3 fighter) and Ki-100 (Type 5)

**Origin:** Kawasaki Kokuki Kogyo.
**Type:** Single-seat fighter.
**Engine:** (Ki-61-I) one 1,175hp Kawasaki Ha-40 inverted-vee 12 liquid-cooled; (Ki-61-II) one 1,450hp Kawasaki Ha-140 of same layout; (Ki-100) one 1,500hp Mitsubishi Ha-112-II 14-cylinder two-row radial.
**Dimensions:** Span 39ft 4½in (12m); length (-I) 29ft 4in (8·94m); (-II) 30ft 0½in (9·16m); (Ki-100) 28ft 11¼in (8·82m); height (all) 12ft 2in (3·7m).
**Weights:** Empty (-I) 5,798lb (2630kg); (-II) 6,294lb (2855kg); (Ki-100) 5,567lb (2525kg); loaded (-I) 7,650lb (3470kg); (-II) 8,433lb (3825kg); (Ki-100) 7,705lb (3495kg).
**Performance:** Maximum speed (-I) 348mph (560km/h); (-II) 379mph (610km/h); (Ki-100) 367mph (590km/h); initial climb (-I, -II) 2,200ft (675m)/min; (Ki-100) 3,280ft (1000m)/min; service ceiling (-I) 32,800ft (10,000m); (-II) 36,089ft (11,000m); (Ki-100) 37,729ft (11,500m); range (-I, -II) 990–1,100 miles (-I, 1800km, -II, 1600km); (Ki-100) 1,243 miles (2000km).
**Armament:** (Ki-61-Ia) two 20mm MG 151/20 in wings, two 7·7mm above engine; (-Id) same but wing guns 30mm; (-IIb) four 20mm Ho-5 in wings; (Ki-100) two Ho-5 in wings and two 12·7mm in fuselage, plus underwing racks for two 551lb (250kg) bombs.
**History:** First flight (Ki-60) March 1941; (Ki-61) December 1941; service delivery (Ki-61-I) August 1942; first flight (-II) August 1943; (Ki-100) 1 February 1945.

**Right:** A Ki-61-IIb bearing the markings of the 2nd Chutai's 244th Sentai (Tokyo defence area, 1945).

**Below:** An early prototype, with Ha-40 engine and original canopy. It was judged the best Army fighter of its day.

Above: Three-view of Ki-61 (interim aircraft with canopy having features of -I and -II and wing of -IIa).

**User:** Japan (Imperial Army).

**Development:** Kawasaki purchased a licence to build the German DB 601 engine in 1937 and the resulting revised and lightened engine emerged in 1940 as the Ha-40. Around this engine Kawasaki planned the Ki-60 and a lighter fighter designated Ki-61. Hien (the Japanese name meaning flying swallow). The latter was completed in December 1941 and flew well, reaching a speed of 368mph. During the first half of 1942 the prototype was extensively tested, performing very well against a captured P-40E and a Bf 109E sent to Japan by submarine. The submarine also brought 800 Mauser MG 151 cannon, and these were fitted to most early Ki-61s despite the unreliability of the supply of electrically fired ammunition. The Gifu

plant delivered 2,654 (according to one authority, 2,750) Ki-61-I and -Ia, the latter being redesigned for easier servicing and increased manoeuvrability. They went into action around New Guinea in April 1943, were called "Tony" by the Allies, and were the only Japanese fighters with a liquid-cooled engine. They were constantly in air combat, later moving to the Philippines and finally back to Japan. By 1944 the Ki-61-II was trickling off the assembly line with an unreliable engine that could not meet production demands. The II had a bigger wing and new canopy, but was soon replaced by the IIa with the old, proven, wing. Only 374 of all -II versions were built, and in early 1945 one of 275 engineless airframes was fitted with the Ha-112 radial. Despite the sudden lash-up conversion the result was a staggeringly fine fighter, easily the best ever produced in Japan. With desperate haste this conversion went into production as the Ki-100. One of the first Ki-100 units destroyed 14 Hellcats without loss to themselves in their first major battle over Okinawa and this easily flown and serviced machine fought supremely well against B-29s and Allied fighters to the end.

# Kyushu K11W Shiragiku

## K11W1 and W2 Shiragiku (White Chrysanthemum)

**Origin:** KK Watanabe Tekkosho (later Kyushu Hikoki KK).
**Type:** Trainer, transport and multi-role utility.
**Engine:** 515hp Hitachi GK2B Amakaze 21 nine-cylinder radial.
**Dimensions:** Span 49ft 1¾in (14·98m); length 33ft 7¼in (10·24m); height 12ft 10¾in (3·931m).
**Weights:** Empty (1) 3,697lb (1677kg); loaded (1) 5,829lb (2644kg), max overload (1) 6,173lb (2800kg).
**Performance:** Maximum speed 139mph (224km/h); range at 106mph (170km/h) as gunnery trainer 730 miles (1175km).
**Armament:** 7·7mm Type 92 manually aimed from rear cockpit, two 66lb (30kg) bombs on underwing racks (as Kamikaze, 551lb, 250kg, bomb under fuselage).
**History:** First flight, November 1942; service delivery, summer 1943; final delivery, August 1945.
**User:** Japan (Imperial Navy).

**Development:** Though one of the commonest aircraft in wartime Japan, the K11W never received an Allied code-name (though such names were allotted to 13 types never used by Japan at all and to 15 types which were pure fiction and never even existed). Obviously based on the North American O-47, this lumbering machine would probably have been better as a twin. In the capacious fuselage were cockpits for the pilot and radio-operator/gunner above the wing, and the instructor, navigator and bomb-aimer below. By VJ-day 798 had been built, a small number at the end of the war

being of the wooden K11W2 type used for transport and ASW. A derived version was the wooden Q3W1 Nankai (South Sea) two-seater with square-tipped wings and tail for ASW use carrying radar and MAD gear. It landed wheels-up in January 1945 and was abandoned.

**Below:** A standard K11W1 after capture. The main entry door is on the left side just behind the trailing edge. So slow a suicide attacker could hardly be effective.

# Kyushu Q1W Tokai "Lorna"

## Q1W1 and W2 Tokai (Eastern Sea) and Q1W1-K Tokai Ren (Eastern Sea Trainer) (Allied code-name "Lorna")

**Origin:** Kyushu Hikoki KK (previously Watanabe).
**Type:** Three-seat ASW aircraft, (-K) four-seat trainer.
**Engines:** Two 610hp Hitachi GK2C Amakaze 31 nine-cylinder radials.
**Dimensions:** Span 52ft 6in (16·00m); length 39ft 8¼in (12·09m); height 13ft 6¼in (4·118m).
**Weights:** Empty 6,839lb (3050kg); loaded 10,582lb (4800kg); max overload 11,755lb (5332kg).
**Performance:** Maximum speed 200mph (322km/h); normal range (315 Imp gal, 1430 litres) 814 miles (1310km), max range (715 Imp gal, 3240 litres) 2,013 miles (3240km).
**Armament:** 7·7mm Type 92 manually aimed from rear cockpit, external fuselage racks for two 551lb (250kg) depth bombs or other stores; provision in nose for two 20mm Type 99 cannon fixed firing ahead or inclined slightly down.
**History:** First flight September 1943; service delivery, late 1944; final delivery August 1945.
**User:** Japan (Imperial Navy).

**Development:** Like other countries, Japan was slow to develop aircraft designed specifically for the vital ASW role. KK Watanabe's design team under Nojiri were assigned to the task under a 17-Shi specification in 1942, but various delays (mainly associated with radar) kept the Q1W away from action until the last year of the war. A straightforward all-metal machine, with constant-speed propellers, the Q1W1 used its hydraulic slotted flaps at 90° to carry out steep diving attacks, and from the start it was pleasant to fly. The crew compartment resembled a Do 17Z or Ju 88, and the usual

**Above: One of the few surviving photographs of a Q1W1. This example was probably finished in pale sea grey, but others were dark olive and even dark blue. Japanese paint schemes were extremely diverse. Note white outline to Hinomaru.**

mission was a low and slow search with naked eyes, though Type 3 ASV and MAD gear were carried. Most operations in 1945 were in Japanese territorial waters, the Korean strait and off Cheju Island, with no confirmed results. Even here many of the 153 built were shot down. The Q1W2 had a wood rear fuselage and the Q1W1-K was all-wood and used for electronic training.

# Mitsubishi A5M "Claude"

## A5M1 to A5M4

**Origin:** Mitsubishi Jukogyo KK; also built by Dai-Nijuichi KK and KK Watanabe Tekkosho.
**Type:** Single-seat carrier-based fighter.
**Engine:** One Nakajima Kotobuki (Jupiter) nine-cylinder radial; (1) 585hp 2-Kai-I; (2) 610hp 2-Kai-3; (4) 710hp Kotobuki 41 or (A5M4 Model 34) 3-Kai.
**Dimensions:** Span (2) 35ft 6in, (4) 36ft 1in (11·0m); length (2) 25ft 7in; (4) 24ft 9½in (7·55m); height 10ft 6in (3·2m).
**Weights:** Empty (2, typical) 2,400lb (1090kg); (4) 2,681lb (1216kg); maximum loaded (2) 3,545lb (1608kg); (4) 3,763lb (1708kg).
**Performance:** Maximum speed (2) 265mph (426km/h); (4) 273mph (440km/h); initial climb (2) 2,215ft (675m)/min; (4) 2,790ft (850m)/min; service ceiling (typical, all) 32,800ft (10,000m); range (2) 460 miles (740km); (4, auxiliary tank) 746 miles (1200km).
**Armament:** (All) two 7·7mm Type 89 machine guns firing on each side of upper cylinder of engine; racks for two 66lb (30kg) bombs under outer wings.
**History:** First flight 4 February 1935; service delivery 1936; final delivery December 1939.
**User:** Japan (Imperial Navy).

**Development:** One of the neatest little warplanes of its day, the A5M was the chief fighter of the Imperial Japanese Navy throughout the Sino-Japanese war and was numerically the most important at the time of Pearl Harbor. It was built to meet a 1934 specification calling for a speed of 218mph

**Below, right: Two of the first A5Ms, probably from the small A5M1 batch, to reach the Chinese theatre in 1937. These turned the tables on the Chinese and achieved complete air supremacy.**

**Below: An A5M2b, with enclosed cockpit. Pilots disliked this feature, and subsequent versions reverted to an open cockpit.**

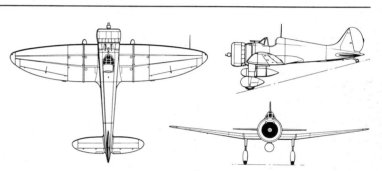

**Above: Three-view of A5M4 with long-range tank.**

and ability to reach 16,400ft in 6½ minutes, and beat these figures by a wide margin. Within days of first flight at Kagamigahara the Ka-14 prototype exceeded 279mph and reached 16,400ft in 5min 54sec, which the Japanese considered "far above the world level at that time". It was the Navy's first monoplane fighter, and one of the first all-metal stressed-skin machines built in Japan. The production A5M1, called Type 96 or S-96 and later given the Allied code name "Claude", abandoned the prototype's inverted-gull wing, originally chosen to try to improve pilot view, and also switched to a direct drive engine. The elliptical wing had split flaps, manoeuvrability was superb and from their first combat mission on 18 September 1937, with the 2nd Combined Air Flotilla based at Shanghai, they acquitted themselves very well. During the conflict with the Soviet Union along the Manchukuo-Mongolian border throughout 1939 the A5M proved the biggest menace to the Russian aircraft, having earlier, on 2 December 1937, destroyed no fewer than ten I-16Bs of the Chinese in one dogfight over Nanking. Such results completely overcame the Naval pilots' earlier distrust of so speedy a monoplane and when the final A5M4 model entered service it was very popular. Mitsubishi built "about 800" (one source states 782), while Kyushu Aircraft (Watanabe) and the Sasebo naval dockyard (D-N) made 200 more. The final version was the A5M4-K dual trainer produced by conversion of fighters in 1941.

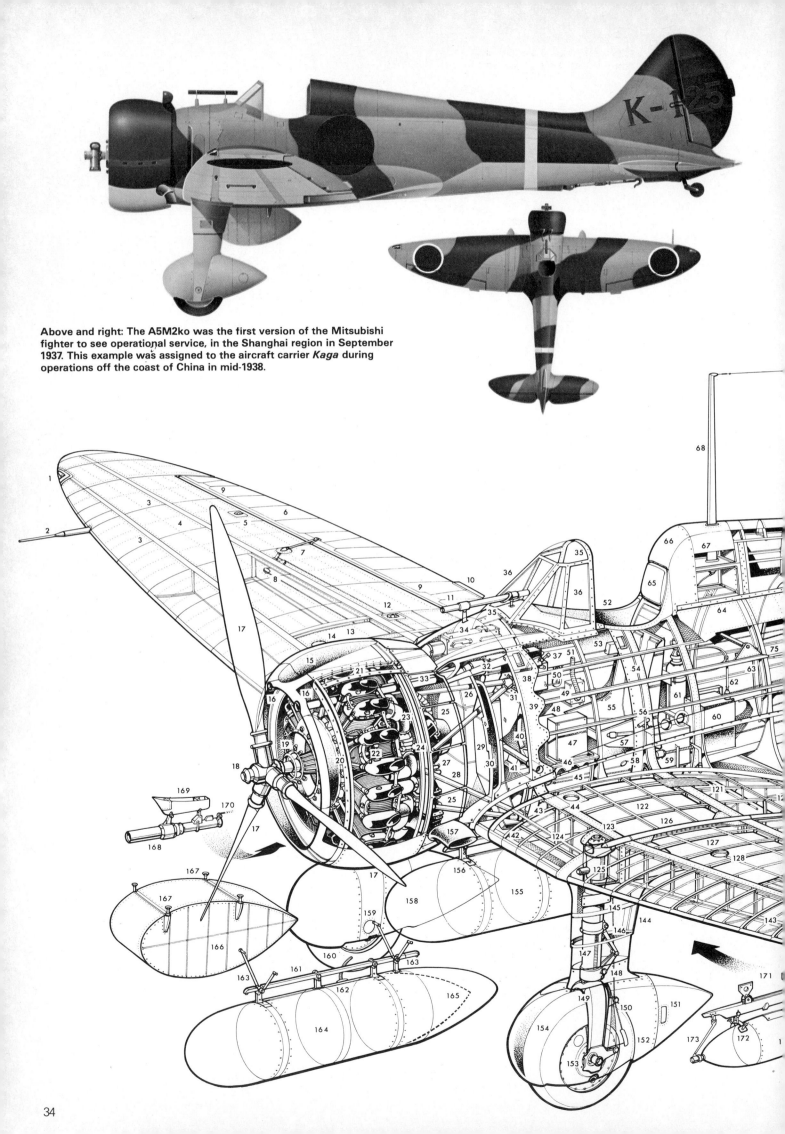

Above and right: The A5M2ko was the first version of the Mitsubishi fighter to see operational service, in the Shanghai region in September 1937. This example was assigned to the aircraft carrier *Kaga* during operations off the coast of China in mid-1938.

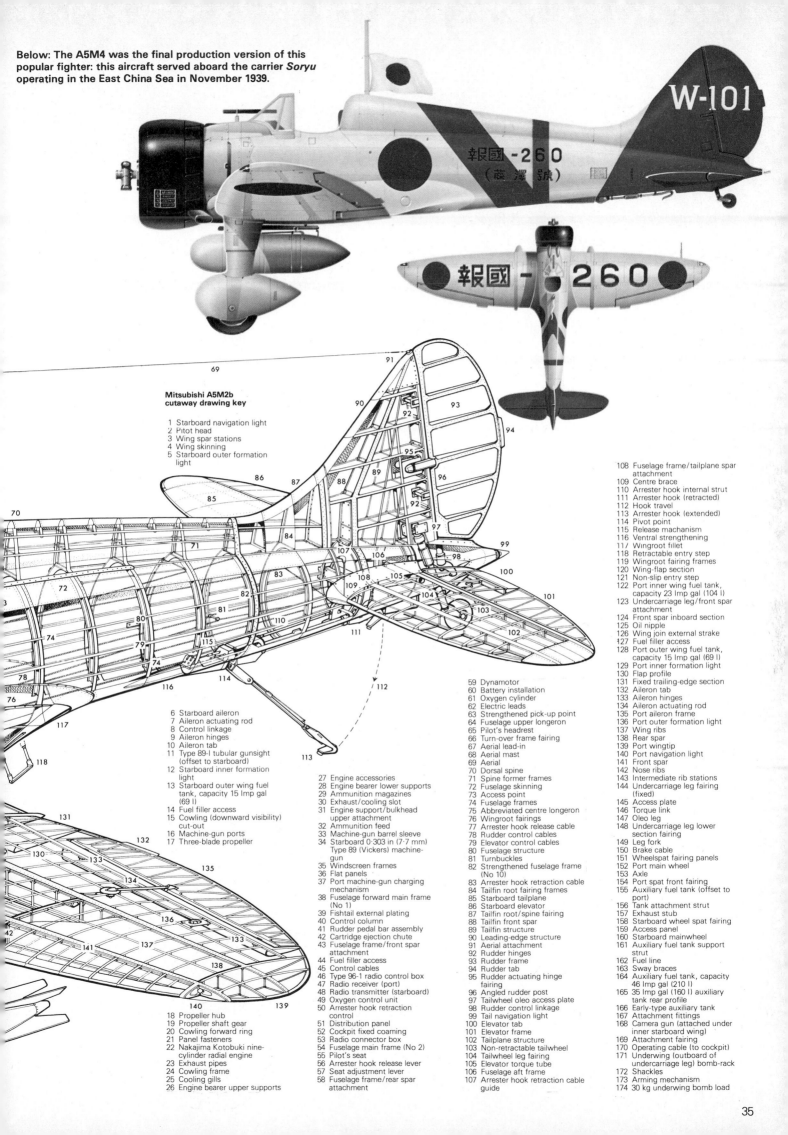

Below: The A5M4 was the final production version of this popular fighter: this aircraft served aboard the carrier *Soryu* operating in the East China Sea in November 1939.

W-101

報國-260
(蔵澤號)

報國-260

**Mitsubishi A5M2b cutaway drawing key**

1 Starboard navigation light
2 Pitot head
3 Wing spar stations
4 Wing skinning
5 Starboard outer formation light
6 Starboard aileron
7 Aileron actuating rod
8 Control linkage
9 Aileron hinges
10 Aileron tab
11 Type 89-I tubular gunsight (offset to starboard)
12 Starboard inner formation light
13 Starboard outer wing fuel tank, capacity 15 Imp gal (69 l)
14 Fuel filler access
15 Cowling (downward visibility) cut-out
16 Machine-gun ports
17 Three-blade propeller
18 Propeller hub
19 Propeller shaft gear
20 Cowling forward ring
21 Panel fasteners
22 Nakajima Kotobuki nine-cylinder radial engine
23 Exhaust pipes
24 Cowling frame
25 Cooling gills
26 Engine bearer upper supports
27 Engine accessories
28 Engine bearer lower supports
29 Ammunition magazines
30 Exhaust/cooling slot
31 Engine support/bulkhead upper attachment
32 Ammunition feed
33 Machine-gun barrel sleeve
34 Starboard 0·303 in (7·7 mm) Type 89 (Vickers) machine-gun
35 Windscreen frames
36 Flat panels
37 Port machine-gun charging mechanism
38 Fuselage forward main frame (No 1)
39 Fishtail external plating
40 Control column
41 Rudder pedal bar assembly
42 Cartridge ejection chute
43 Fuselage frame/front spar attachment
44 Fuel filler access
45 Control cables
46 Type 96-1 radio control box
47 Radio receiver (port)
48 Radio transmitter (starboard)
49 Oxygen control unit
50 Arrester hook retraction control
51 Distribution panel
52 Cockpit fixed coaming
53 Radio connector box
54 Fuselage main frame (No 2)
55 Pilot's seat
56 Arrester hook release lever
57 Seat adjustment lever
58 Fuselage frame/rear spar attachment
59 Dynamotor
60 Battery installation
61 Oxygen cylinder
62 Electric leads
63 Strengthened pick-up point
64 Fuselage upper longeron
65 Pilot's headrest
66 Turn-over frame fairing
67 Aerial lead-in
68 Aerial mast
69 Aerial
70 Dorsal spine
71 Spine former frames
72 Fuselage skinning
73 Access point
74 Fuselage frames
75 Abbreviated centre longeron
76 Wingroot fairings
77 Arrester hook release cable
78 Rudder control cables
79 Elevator control cables
80 Fuselage structure
81 Turnbuckles
82 Strengthened fuselage frame (No 10)
83 Arrester hook retraction cable
84 Tailfin root fairing frames
85 Starboard tailplane
86 Starboard elevator
87 Tailfin root/spine fairing
88 Tailfin front spar
89 Tailfin structure
90 Leading-edge structure
91 Aerial attachment
92 Rudder hinges
93 Rudder frame
94 Rudder tab
95 Rudder actuating hinge fairing
96 Angled rudder post
97 Tailwheel oleo access plate
98 Rudder control linkage
99 Tail navigation light
100 Elevator tab
101 Elevator frame
102 Tailplane structure
103 Non-retractable tailwheel
104 Tailwheel leg fairing
105 Elevator torque tube
106 Fuselage aft frame
107 Arrester hook retraction cable guide
108 Fuselage frame/tailplane spar attachment
109 Centre brace
110 Arrester hook internal strut
111 Arrester hook (retracted)
112 Hook travel
113 Arrester hook (extended)
114 Pivot point
115 Release mechanism
116 Ventral strengthening
117 Wingroot fillet
118 Retractable entry step
119 Wingroot fairing frames
120 Wing-flap section
121 Non-slip entry step
122 Port inner wing fuel tank, capacity 23 Imp gal (104 l)
123 Undercarriage leg/front spar attachment
124 Front spar inboard section
125 Oil nipple
126 Wing join external strake
127 Fuel filler access
128 Port outer wing fuel tank, capacity 15 Imp gal (69 l)
129 Port inner formation light
130 Flap profile
131 Fixed trailing-edge section
132 Aileron tab
133 Aileron hinges
134 Aileron actuating rod
135 Port aileron frame
136 Port outer formation light
137 Wing ribs
138 Rear spar
139 Port wingtip
140 Port navigation light
141 Front spar
142 Nose ribs
143 Intermediate rib stations
144 Undercarriage leg fairing (fixed)
145 Access plate
146 Torque link
147 Oleo leg
148 Undercarriage leg lower section fairing
149 Leg fork
150 Brake cable
151 Wheelspat fairing panels
152 Port main wheel
153 Axle
154 Port spat front fairing
155 Auxiliary fuel tank (offset to port)
156 Tank attachment strut
157 Exhaust stub
158 Starboard wheel spat fairing
159 Access panel
160 Starboard mainwheel
161 Auxiliary fuel tank support strut
162 Fuel line
163 Sway braces
164 Auxiliary fuel tank, capacity 46 Imp gal (210 l)
165 35 Imp gal (160 l) auxiliary tank rear profile
166 Early-type auxiliary tank
167 Attachment fittings
168 Camera gun (attached under inner starboard wing)
169 Attachment fairing
170 Operating cable (to cockpit)
171 Underwing (outboard of undercarriage leg) bomb-rack
172 Shackles
173 Arming mechanism
174 30 kg underwing bomb load

# Mitsubishi A6M Zero-Sen "Zeke"

## A6M1 to A6M8c and Nakajima A6M2-N

**Origin:** Mitsubishi Jukogyo KK; also built by Nakajima Hikoki KK.

**Type:** Single-seat carrier-based fighter, (A6M2-N) float seaplane.

**Engine:** (A6M1) one 780hp Mitsubishi MK2 Zuisei 13 14-cylinder two-row radial: (M2) 925hp Nakajima NK1C Sakae 12 of same layout; (M3) 1,130hp Sakae 21; (M5) as M3 with individual exhaust stacks; (M6c) Sakae 31 with same rated power but water/methanol boost to 1,210hp for emergency; (M8c) 1,560hp Mitsubishi Kinsei 62 of same layout.

**Dimensions:** Span (1, 2) 39ft 4½in (12·0m); (remainder) 36ft 1in (11·0m); length (all landplanes) 29ft 9in (9·06m); (A6M2-N) 33ft 2¾in (10·13m); height (1, 2) 9ft 7in (2·92m); (all later landplanes) 9ft 8in (2·98m); (A6M2-N) 14ft 1¼in (4·3m).

**Weights:** Empty (2) 3,704lb (1680kg); (3) 3,984lb (1807kg); (5) typically 3,920lb (1778kg); (6c) 4,175lb (1894kg); (8c) 4,740lb (2150kg); (A6M2-N) 3,968lb (1800kg); maximum loaded (2) 5,313lb (2410kg); (3) 5,828lb (2644kg); (5c) 6,050lb (2733kg; 2952kg as overload); (6c) as 5c; (8c) 6,944lb (3149kg); (A6M2-N) 5,423lb (2460kg).

**Performance:** Maximum speed (2) 316mph (509km/h); (3) 336mph (541km/h); (5c, 6c) 354mph (570km/h); (8c) 360mph (580km/h); (A6M2-N) 273mph (440km/h); initial climb (1, 2, 3) 4,500ft (1370m)/min; (5, 6c) 3,150ft (960m)/min; (2-N) not known; service ceiling (1, 2) 33,790ft (10,300m); (3) 36,250ft (11,050m); (5c, 6c) 37,500ft (11,500m); (8c) 39,370ft (12,000m); (A6M2-N) 32,800ft (10,000m); range with drop tank (2) 1,940 miles (3110km); (5) 1,200 miles (1920km).

**Armament:** (1, 2, 3 and 2-N) two 20mm Type 99 cannon each with 60-round drum fixed in outer wings, two 7·7mm Type 97 machine guns each

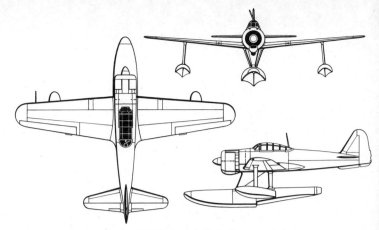

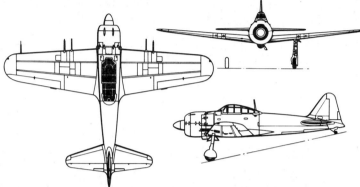

Above: Three-view of A6M2-N, by Nakajima.

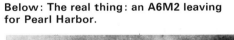

Above: Three-view of A6M5c, which introduced the final armament but was severely underpowered with unboosted engine.

Left: Nearly all these are the A6M5 Model 52 variant.

with 500 rounds above front fuselage, and wing racks for two 66lb (30kg) bombs; (5a) two 20mm Type 99 Mk 4 with belt of 85 rounds per gun, two 7·7mm in fuselage and wing racks for two 132lb (60kg) bombs; (5b) as 5a but one 7·7mm replaced by 12·7mm; (5c and all later versions) two 20mm Type 99 Mk 4 and two 13·2mm in wings, one 13·2mm (optional) in fuselage, plus wing racks for two 60kg.

**History:** First flight 1 April 1939; service delivery (A6M1) late July 1940; first flight (A6M2-N) December 1941; (A6M5) August 1943; (A6M2-K) January 1942.

**User:** Japan (Imperial Navy).

**Development:** The most famous of all Japanese combat aircraft possessed the unique distinction of being the first carrier-based fighter ever to outperform corresponding land-based machines; it was also a singularly unpleasant shock to US and British staff which had apparently never studied

Below: How a Japanese artist saw early-model A6M2 Model 21 Zero-Sens on a carrier flight deck (probably aboard Zuikaku before Pearl Harbor).

Below: The real thing: an A6M2 leaving for Pearl Harbor.

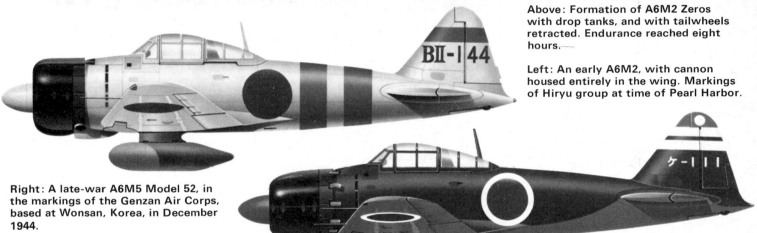

**Above: Formation of A6M2 Zeros with drop tanks, and with tailwheels retracted. Endurance reached eight hours.**

**Left: An early A6M2, with cannon housed entirely in the wing. Markings of Hiryu group at time of Pearl Harbor.**

**Right: A late-war A6M5 Model 52, in the markings of the Genzan Air Corps, based at Wonsan, Korea, in December 1944.**

**Below: A neat stepped-up echelon of the A6M2-N floatplane version, which was outclassed as an air-combat fighter.**

the behaviour of this fighter in China or even discovered its existence. It was designed by Mitsubishi to meet the severe demands of the 1937 Navy carrier-based fighter specification, seeking a successor to the A5M. Demands included a speed of 500km/h (311mph) and armament of two cannon and two machine guns. Under team leader Jiro Horikoshi the new fighter took shape as a clean, efficient but lightly built aircraft with outstanding manoeuvrability. With a more powerful engine it was accepted for production as the A6M2, though as it was put into production in 1940, the Japanese year 5700, it became popularly the Zero-Sen (Type 00 fighter), and to millions of its enemies was simply the "Zero" (though the official Allied code name was "Zeke"). Before official trials were completed two squadrons with 15 aircraft were sent to China in July 1940 for trials under operational conditions. They eliminated all opposition, as forcefully reported to Washington by Gen Claire Chennault, commander of the Flying Tigers volunteer force (his warning was obviously filed before being read). More than 400 had been delivered by the time the A6M2 and clipped-wing M3 appeared at Pearl Harbor. During the subsequent year it seemed that thousands of these fighters were in use, their unrivalled manoeuvrability being matched by unparalleled range with a small engine, 156gal internal fuel and drop tanks. So completely did the A6M sweep away Allied air power that the Japanese nation came to believe it was invincible. After the Battle of Midway the Allies slowly gained the ascendancy, and the A6M found itself outclassed by the F4U and F6F. Mitsubishi urgently tried to devise improved versions and the A6M5 was built in quantities far greater than any other Japanese combat aircraft. Improvements were mainly small and the combat-boosted Sakae 31 engine did not appear until the end of 1944. Only a few of the much more powerful A6M8c type

were produced, the main reason for this change of engine being destruction of the Nakajima factory. The final model was the A6M7 Kamikaze version, though hundreds of Zeros of many sub-types were converted for suicide attacks. Total production amounted to 10,937, of which 6,217 were built by Nakajima which also designed and built 327 of the attractive A6M2-N single-float seaplane fighter version (code name "Rufe") which operated throughout the Pacific war. The A6M2-K was one of several dual trainer versions.

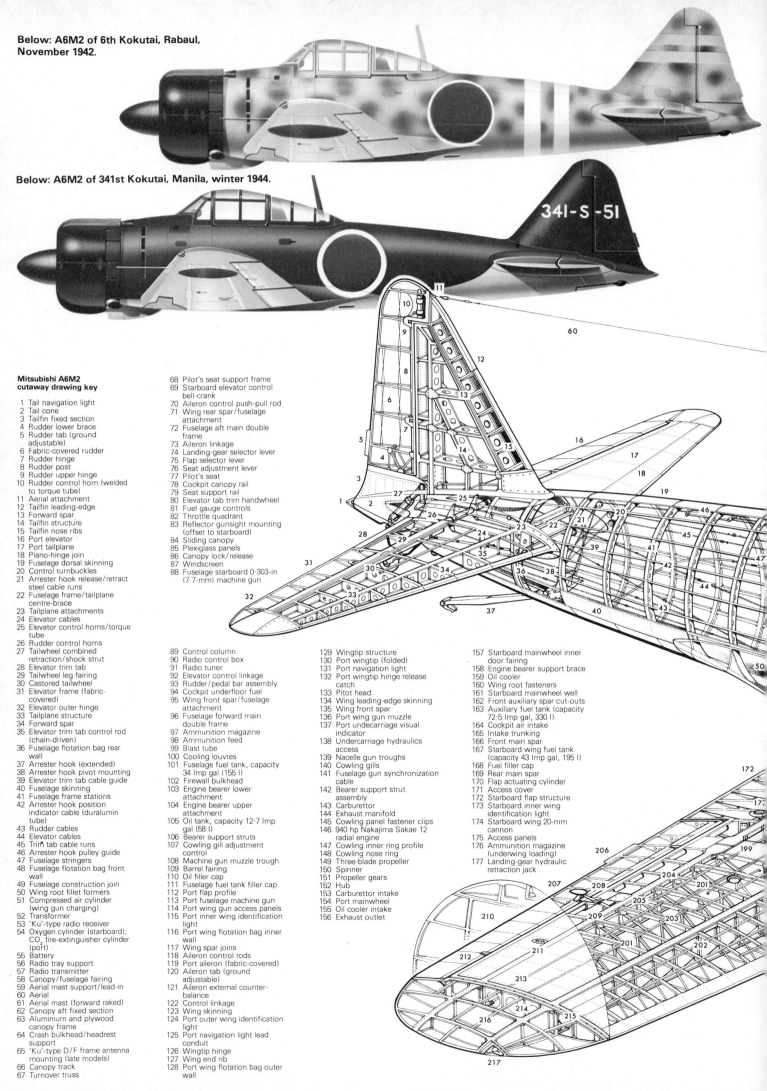

**Below: A6M2 of 6th Kokutai, Rabaul, November 1942.**

**Below: A6M2 of 341st Kokutai, Manila, winter 1944.**

341-S-51

**Mitsubishi A6M2 cutaway drawing key**

1 Tail navigation light
2 Tail cone
3 Tailfin fixed section
4 Rudder lower brace
5 Rudder tab (ground adjustable)
6 Fabric-covered rudder
7 Rudder hinge
8 Rudder post
9 Rudder upper hinge
10 Rudder control horn (welded to torque tube)
11 Aerial attachment
12 Tailfin leading-edge
13 Forward spar
14 Tailfin structure
15 Tailfin nose ribs
16 Port elevator
17 Port tailplane
18 Piano-hinge join
19 Fuselage dorsal skinning
20 Control turnbuckles
21 Arrester hook release/retract steel cable runs
22 Fuselage frame/tailplane centre-brace
23 Tailplane attachments
24 Elevator cables
25 Elevator control horns/torque tube
26 Rudder control horns
27 Tailwheel combined retraction/shock strut
28 Elevator trim tab
29 Tailwheel leg fairing
30 Castored tailwheel
31 Elevator frame (fabric-covered)
32 Elevator outer hinge
33 Tailplane structure
34 Forward spar
35 Elevator trim tab control rod (chain-driven)
36 Fuselage flotation bag rear wall
37 Arrester hook (extended)
38 Arrester hook pivot mounting
39 Elevator trim tab cable guide
40 Fuselage skinning
41 Fuselage frame stations
42 Arrester hook position indicator cable (duralumin tube)
43 Rudder cables
44 Elevator cables
45 Trim tab cable runs
46 Arrester hook pulley guide
47 Fuselage stringers
48 Fuselage flotation bag front wall
49 Fuselage construction join
50 Wing root fillet formers
51 Compressed air cylinder (wing gun charging)
52 Transformer
53 'Ku'-type radio receiver
54 Oxygen cylinder (starboard); CO₂ fire-extinguisher cylinder (port)
55 Battery
56 Radio tray support
57 Radio transmitter
58 Canopy/fuselage fairing
59 Aerial mast support/lead-in
60 Aerial
61 Aerial mast (forward raked)
62 Canopy aft fixed section
63 Aluminium and plywood canopy frame
64 Crash bulkhead/headrest support
65 'Ku'-type D/F frame antenna mounting (late models)
66 Canopy track
67 Turnover truss
68 Pilot's seat support frame
69 Starboard elevator control bell-crank
70 Aileron control push-pull rod
71 Wing rear spar/fuselage attachment
72 Fuselage aft main double frame
73 Aileron linkage
74 Landing-gear selector lever
75 Flap selector lever
76 Seat adjustment lever
77 Pilot's seat
78 Cockpit canopy rail
79 Seat support rail
80 Elevator tab trim handwheel
81 Fuel gauge controls
82 Throttle quadrant
83 Reflector gunsight mounting (offset to starboard)
84 Sliding canopy
85 Plexiglass panels
86 Canopy lock/release
87 Windscreen
88 Fuselage starboard 0·303-in (7·7-mm) machine gun
89 Control column
90 Radio control box
91 Radio tuner
92 Elevator control linkage
93 Rudder/pedal bar assembly
94 Cockpit underfloor fuel
95 Wing front spar/fuselage attachment
96 Fuselage forward main double frame
97 Ammunition magazine
98 Ammunition feed
99 Blast tube
100 Cooling louvres
101 Fuselage fuel tank, capacity 34 Imp gal (155 l)
102 Firewall bulkhead
103 Engine bearer lower attachment
104 Engine bearer upper attachment
105 Oil tank, capacity 12·7 Imp gal (58 l)
106 Bearer support struts
107 Cowling gill adjustment control
108 Machine gun muzzle trough
109 Barrel fairing
110 Oil filler cap
111 Fuselage fuel tank filler cap
112 Port flap profile
113 Port fuselage machine gun
114 Port wing gun access panels
115 Port inner wing identification light
116 Port wing flotation bag inner wall
117 Wing spar joins
118 Aileron control rods
119 Port aileron (fabric-covered)
120 Aileron tab (ground adjustable)
121 Aileron external counter-balance
122 Control linkage
123 Wing skinning
124 Port outer wing identification light
125 Port navigation light lead conduit
126 Wingtip hinge
127 Wing end rib
128 Port wing flotation bag outer wall
129 Wingtip structure
130 Port wingtip (folded)
131 Port navigation light
132 Port wingtip hinge release catch
133 Pitot head
134 Wing leading-edge skinning
135 Wing front spar
136 Port wing gun muzzle
137 Port undercarriage visual indicator
138 Undercarriage hydraulics access
139 Nacelle gun troughs
140 Cowling gills
141 Fuselage gun synchronization cable
142 Bearer support strut assembly
143 Carburettor
144 Exhaust manifold
145 Cowling panel fastener clips
146 940 hp Nakajima Sakae 12 radial engine
147 Cowling inner ring profile
148 Cowling nose ring
149 Three-blade propeller
150 Spinner
151 Propeller gears
152 Hub
153 Carburettor intake
154 Port mainwheel
155 Oil cooler intake
156 Exhaust outlet
157 Starboard mainwheel inner door fairing
158 Engine bearer support brace
159 Oil cooler
160 Wing root fasteners
161 Starboard mainwheel well
162 Front auxiliary spar cut-outs
163 Auxiliary fuel tank (capacity 72·5 Imp gal, 330 l)
164 Cockpit air intake
165 Intake trunking
166 Front main spar
167 Starboard wing fuel tank (capacity 43 Imp gal, 195 l)
168 Fuel filler cap
169 Rear main spar
170 Flap actuating cylinder
171 Access cover
172 Starboard flap structure
173 Starboard inner wing identification light
174 Starboard wing 20-mm cannon
175 Access panels
176 Ammunition magazine (underwing loading)
177 Landing-gear hydraulic retraction jack

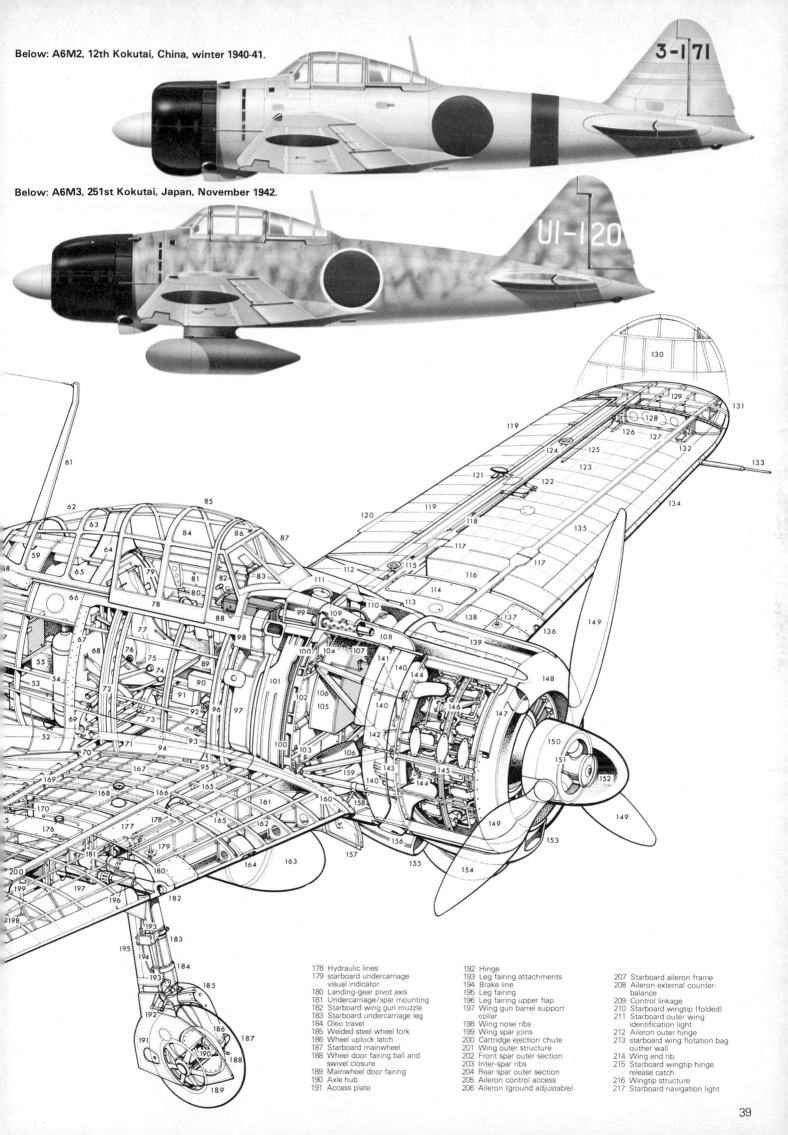

Below: A6M2, 12th Kokutai, China, winter 1940-41.

3-171

Below: A6M3, 251st Kokutai, Japan, November 1942.

UI-120

178 Hydraulic lines
179 starboard undercarriage visual indicator
180 Landing-gear pivot axis
181 Undercarriage/spar mounting
182 Starboard wing gun muzzle
183 Starboard undercarriage leg
184 Oleo travel
185 Welded steel wheel fork
186 Wheel uplock latch
187 Starboard mainwheel
188 Wheel door fairing ball and swivel closure
189 Mainwheel door fairing
190 Axle hub
191 Access plate

192 Hinge
193 Leg fairing attachments
194 Brake line
195 Leg fairing
196 Leg fairing upper flap
197 Wing gun barrel support collar
198 Wing nose ribs
199 Wing spar joins
200 Cartridge ejection chute
201 Wing outer structure
202 Front spar outer section
203 Inter-spar ribs
204 Rear spar outer section
205 Aileron control access
206 Aileron (ground adjustable)

207 Starboard aileron frame
208 Aileron external counter-balance
209 Control linkage
210 Starboard wingtip (folded)
211 Starboard outer wing identification light
212 Aileron outer hinge
213 starboard wing flotation bag outher wall
214 Wing end rib
215 Starboard wingtip hinge release catch
216 Wingtip structure
217 Starboard navigation light

39

# Mitsubishi F1M "Pete"

### F1M1, F1M2

**Origin:** Mitsubishi Jukogyo KK; also built by Dai-Nijuichi KK (Sasebo).
**Type:** Design role, reconnaissance (but see text).
**Engine:** (1) one 820hp Nakajima Hikari 1 nine-cylinder radial; (2) one 875hp Mitsubishi Zuisei 13 14-cylinder two-row radial.
**Dimensions:** Span 36ft 1in (11·0m); length 31ft 2in (9·5m); height 13ft 1½in (4·0m).
**Weights:** (2) empty 4,330lb (1964kg); normal loaded 5,620lb (2550kg); maximum overload 6,296lb (2856kg).
**Performance:** Maximum speed 230mph (370km/h); initial climb 1,969ft (600m)/min; service ceiling 30,970ft (9440m); range (normal weight) 276 miles (445km), (overload) 670 miles (1070km).
**Armament:** Two 7·7mm Type 89 fixed above engine, one manually aimed from rear cockpit; underwing racks for two 132lb (60kg) bombs or one 250kg (551lb).
**History:** First flight (F1M1 prototype) June 1936; (production F1M2) October 1939; service delivery 1941; final delivery March 1944.
**User:** Japan (Imperial Navy).

**Development:** At first glance a small observation biplane for catapulting from surface vessels might seem hardly to rank as much of a warplane, but in fact the F1M served throughout World War II in such roles as area-defence fighter, bomber, convoy escort, anti-submarine attack aircraft,

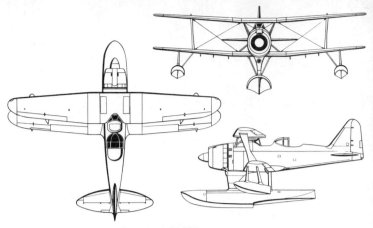

Above: Three-view of typical F1M2.

ocean patrol, rescue and even transport. It was in 1934 that the Imperial Japanese Navy issued a requirement for a new shipboard reconnaissance machine to succeed the Nakajima E8N (code name "Dave"). Mitsubishi's design team, led by Eitaro Sano, won over Aichi and Kawanishi rivals (using "Dave"-type floats) and notable features of the F1M1 were extreme attention to detail cleanliness and exceptional manoeuvrability at all speeds.

---

# Mitsubishi G3M "Nell"

### G3M1, G3M2 and G3M3; some rebuilt as L3Y

**Origin:** Mitsubishi Jukogyo KK, Nagoya; also built by Nakajima Hikoki KK at Koizumi.
**Type:** Long-range land-based bomber (L3Y, transport).
**Engines:** Two Mitsubishi Kinsei 14-cylinder two-row radials, (G3M1, L3Y1) 910hp Kinsei 3, (G3M2, L3Y2) 1,075hp Kinsei 42 or 45, (G3M3) 1,300hp Kinsei 51.
**Dimensions:** Span 82ft 0¼in (25·00m); length 53ft 11½in (16·45m); height 12ft 1in (3·685m).
**Weights:** Empty (1) 10,516lb (4770kg), (3) 11,551lb (5243kg); max loaded (1) 16,848lb (7642kg), (3) 17,637lb (8000kg).
**Performance:** Maximum speed (1) 216mph (348km/h), (2) 232mph (373km/h), (3) 258mph (415km/h); service ceiling (3) 33,730ft (10,280 m); maximum range (3) 3,871 miles (6228km).
**Armament:** (1 and 2) up to four 7·7mm Type 92 manually aimed from two retractable dorsal positions, ventral position and cockpit, (3) one 20mm Type 99 in dorsal fairing and three 7·7mm in side blisters, cockpit and ventral position; external bomb load or torpedo of 1,764lb (800kg).
**History:** First flight (Ka-15 prototype) July 1935; service delivery late 1936.
**User:** Imperial Japanese Navy.

**Development:** Derived from the Ka-9 of April 1934, the Ka-15 series of prototypes were among the first outstanding Japanese warplanes superior to Western types. Designed by a team under Prof Kiro Honjo, the Ka-15 was a smooth stressed-skin machine, with exceptional range. On 14 August 1937 the Kanoya air corps based on Taipei made the world's first trans-oceanic raid when a large force of G3M2 hit targets 1,250 miles away in China. Many other great raids were made, but the most famous action was the sinking of HMS *Prince of Wales* and *Repulse* (which thought they were out of range) on 10 December 1941. By 1943 most were in second-line service, though known to the Allies as "Nell". The L3Y transport conversion was code-named "Tina".

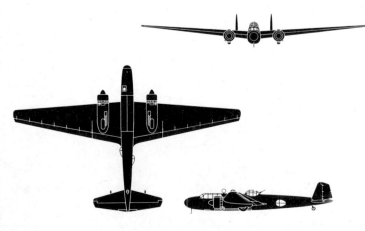

Above: Three-view of G3M3 Model 23 (G3M2 similar).

Above: Mitsubishi G3M2 bombers, probably of the Mihoro Kokutai, photographed whilst releasing their bombs in a stick. All aircraft in the picture are of the Model 22 sub-type with a large turtle-back dorsal gun position equipped with a 20mm cannon. The Mihoro Kokutai provided high-level bombers which sank the British capital ships *Prince of Wales* and *Repulse* on 10 December 1941.

Left: Side elevation of the F1M2 seen in the photograph below. The designation was Navy Type 0 observation seaplane Model 11. The painted float-band warns of the propeller disc.

Below: F1M2 seaplanes of the "P3" unit operated from sandy beaches on south-west Pacific islands.

After protracted development to improve stability, with the elliptical wings made straight-tapered and the tail enlarged, the floats and the engine changed, the F1M2 version went into production. Altogether 1,118 were delivered, including 590 made at the Navy arsenal at Sasebo. For a while the Allies, who code-named it "Pete", thought the F1M a Sasebo design. "Petes" were active in dogfights in the Aleutians, Solomons and many other campaigns; almost the only thing they found difficult to do effectively was deliver 551lb bombs.

# Mitsubishi G4M "Betty"

## G4M1 to G4M3c and G6M

**Origin:** Mitsubishi Jukogyo KK.
**Type:** Land-based naval torpedo bomber and missile carrier.
**Engines:** (G4M1) two 1,530hp Mitsubishi Kasei 11 14-cylinder two-row radials; (subsequent versions) two Kasei 22 rated at 1,850hp with water/methanol injection.
**Dimensions:** Span 81ft 7¾in (24·89m); length (1) 65ft 6¼in; (later versions) 64ft 4¾in (19·63m); height (1) 16ft 1in; (later versions) 13ft 5¾in (4·11m).
**Weights:** Empty (1) 14,860lb (6741kg); (2) 17,623lb (7994kg); (3) 18,500lb (8391kg); loaded (1) 20,944lb (9500kg); (2, 3) 27,550lb (12,500kg); max overload (1) 28,350lb (12,860kg); (2, 3) 33,070lb (15,000kg).
**Performance:** Maximum speed (1) 265mph (428km/h); (2) 271mph (437km/h); (3) 283mph (455km/h); initial climb (1) 1,800ft (550m)/min; (2, 3) 1,380ft (420m)/min; service ceiling (all) about 30,000ft (9144m); range (with bombs at overload weight) (1) 3,132 miles (5040km); (2) 2,982 miles (4800km); (3) 2,262 miles (3640km).
**Armament:** (1) three manually aimed 7·7mm in nose, dorsal and ventral positions and 20mm manually aimed in tail; internal bomb load of 2,205lb (1000kg) or 1,764lb (800kg) torpedo externally; (2) as before but electric dorsal turret (one 7·7mm) and revised tail position with increased arc of fire; (2e, and, retro-actively, many earlier G4M2) one 7·7mm in nose, one 20mm in dorsal turret and manual 20mm in tail and two beam windows. (G4M2e) adapted to carry Ohka piloted missile.
**History:** First flight October 1939; service delivery April 1941; first flight (G4M2) November 1942.
**User:** Japan (Imperial Navy).

**Development:** Designed to an incredibly difficult 1938 Navy specification, the G4M family (Allied name, "Betty") was the Imperial Japanese Navy's premier heavy bomber in World War II; yet the insistence on the great range of 2,000 nautical miles (3706km) with full bomb load made the saving of weight take priority over defence and the aircraft was highly vulnerable and not very popular. The wing was of the same Mitsubishi 118 section as the Zero-Sen and boldly designed as an integral fuel tank to accommodate no less than 5,000 litres (1,100gal). The company kept recommending four engines and being overruled by the Navy, which, during the early flight-test stage, wasted more than a year, and 30 aircraft, in trying to make the design into the G6M bomber escort with crew of ten and 19 guns. Eventually the G4M1 was readied for service as a bomber and flew its first missions in South East China in May 1941. More than 250 operated in the Philippines and Malayan campaigns, but after the Solomons battle in August 1942 it began to be apparent that, once intercepted and hit, the unprotected

**Above: Three-view of G4M2, without bulged weapon-bay doors.**

bomber went up like a torch (hence the Allied nickname "one-shot lighter"). Total production reached the exceptional quantity of 2,479, most of them in the many sub-types of G4M2 with increased fuel capacity and power. Finally the trend of development was reversed with the G4M3 series with full protection and only 968gal fuel.

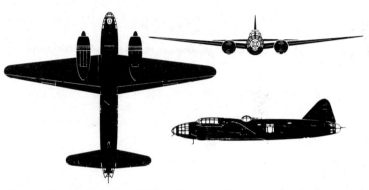

**Above: Formation of variously coloured G4M1 bombers, probably operating over China in 1941 when the aircraft were new.**

**Left: A G4M2a of the 763rd Kokutai (Air Corps). This aircraft was found abandoned in the Philippines. Finish was dark green above and natural metal on underside.**

# Mitsubishi J2M Raiden "Jack"

## J2M1 to J2M7

**Origin:** Mitsubishi Jukogyo KK; also small number (J2M5) built by Koza Kaigun Kokusho.

**Type:** Single-seat Navy land-based interceptor.

**Engine:** Most versions, one 1,820hp Mitsubishi MK4R-A Kasei 23a 14-cylinder two-row radial; (J2M5) 1,820hp MK4U-A Kasei 26a.

**Dimensions:** Span 35ft 5¼in (10·8m); length (most) 31ft 9¾in (9·70m); (J2M5) 32ft 7⅜in (9·95m); height (most) 12ft 6in (3·81m); (J2M5) 12ft 11¼in (3·94m).

**Weights:** Empty (2) 5,572lb (2527kg); (3) 5,675lb (2574kg); (5) 6,259lb (2839kg); normal loaded (2) 7,257lb (3300kg); (3) 7,573lb (3435kg); (5) 7,676lb (3482kg); max overload (2, 3) 8,700lb (3946kg).

**Performance:** Maximum speed (2) 371mph (596km/h); (3) 380mph (612km/h); (5) 382mph (615km/h); initial climb (2, 3) 3,610ft (1100m)/min; (5) 3,030ft (925m)/min; range (2, 3 at normal gross) 655 miles (1055km); (2, 3 overload) 1,580 miles (2520km); (5, normal gross with 30min reserve) 345 miles (555km).

**Armament:** See text.

**History:** First flight (prototype) 20 March 1942; service delivery (J2M2) December 1943; first flight (J2M5) May 1944.

**User:** Japan (Imperial Navy).

**Development:** Though designed by a team led by the legendary Jiro Horikoshi, creator of the Zero-Sen, this utterly different little interceptor did little to enhance reputations, though there was nothing fundamentally faulty in its conception. It broke totally new ground, partly in being an interceptor for the Navy (previously the preserve of the Army) and partly in the reversal of design parameters. Instead of concentrating on combat manoeuvrability at all costs the J1M was designed solely for speed and fast climb. Manoeuvrability and even handling took second place. Unusual features in the basic design included a tiny laminar-flow wing fitted with combat flaps, a finely streamlined engine with propeller extension shaft and fan cooling, a very shallow enclosed canopy and a surprising number of forged parts in the stressed-skin airframe. Powered by a 1,460hp Kasei, the

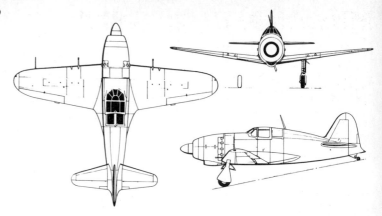

**Above: Three-view of J2M3.**

prototype Mitsubishi M-20, named Raiden (Thunderbolt), gave a great deal of trouble and was almost redesigned to produce the J2M2 with different engine, much deeper canopy, multi-stack exhaust and new four-blade propeller. Even then the Raiden suffered endless snags and crashes, but eventually 155 J2M2 were delivered with two 20mm Type 99 and two 7·7mm above the fuselage. Production then switched to the J2M3 with machine guns removed and the wing fitted with two Type 99 and two fast-firing Type 99-II. The J2M3a had four Type 99-II. Fitted with bulged canopy these models became the J2M6 and 6a. A few high-flying J2M4 turbocharged versions were built, with six cannon, the two added guns being in the top fuselage decking. Best of all was the J2M5 with only two (wing) cannon but a far better engine, and it proved formidable against high-flying B-29s. After VJ-day, when only 480 of all models had been built by Mitsubishi (one month's planned output!), the Allies (who called this fighter "Jack") spoke in glowing terms of its performance and handling.

**Right: A J2M, probably a J2M3a Raiden 21a, of the 302nd Air Corps. This type had four Type 99-II cannon, faster-firing than the guns fitted to earlier models of this fighter.**

# Mitsubishi Ki-15 "Babs"

## Ki-15-I, Ki-15-II, C5M, Karigane

**Origin:** Mitsubishi Jukogyo KK.

**Type:** Two-seat light attack bomber.

**Engine:** (I) one 750hp Nakajima Ha-8 nine-cylinder radial; (II) one 800hp Mitsubishi A.14 (later named Kinsei) 14-cylinder two-row radial.

**Dimensions:** Span 39ft 4¼in (12·0m); length (I) 27ft 11in (8·50m); height 9ft 10in (3·0m).

**Weights:** Empty (I) 3,968lb (1800kg); maximum loaded (I) 5,070lb (2300kg); (II) 6,834lb (3100kg).

**Performance:** Maximum speed (I) 280mph (450km/h); (II) about 298mph (480km/h); initial climb (both) about 1,640ft (500m)/min; service ceiling (I) 28,220ft (8600m); range with bomb load (both) about 1,100 miles (1800km).

**Armament:** One 7·7mm Type 89 (not always fitted) fixed in outer wing firing forward, and one manually aimed from rear cockpit; bomb load of up to 551lb (250kg) in (I) or 1,100lb (500kg) in (II) carried externally.

**History:** First flight (Karigane prototype) May 1936; (Ki-15-I) probably late 1936.

**User:** Imperial Japanese Army.

**Development:** This trim little machine stemmed from a private venture by the giant Mitsubishi company, inspired by the emergence in the United States of modern stressed-skin monoplanes (particularly the Northrop A-17). With company funds, but sponsored by the Asahi (Rising Sun) newspaper, a prototype was built to demonstrate the ability of the fast-growing Japanese industry to build modern aircraft. It was a time of intense nationalism and the resulting machine, named Karigane (Wild Goose) by Mitsubishi, was individually christened "Kamikaze" (Divine Wind) and prepared as an instrument of national publicity. Its greatest achievement was a notably trouble-free flight of 9,900 miles from Tokyo to London in April 1937. Others were built for similar purposes (one being "Asakaze" (Morning Wind) of the Asahi Press) and as fast mailplanes, while in 1938 a small batch was built with the 550hp Kotobuki (licence-built Bristol Jupiter) replaced by the much more powerful A.14 engine. In 1937 construction began of 437 military Ki-15 series for the Army and these were soon one of the first really modern types to go into action in the Sino-Japanese war, which had simmered for years and finally broke out in 1937. The Ki-15 was used for level bombing, close support and photo-reconnaissance, but was replaced by the Ki-30 (p. 156). In 1939 the Imperial Navy began to receive 50 of two C5M versions with different engines. Allied code name was "Babs".

**Left: A Mitsubishi Ki-15-I of the 1st Chutai, 15th Hikosentai, of the Imperial Army. When the second Sino-Japanese war broke out in 1937 the Ki-15 was one of the first types to go into action. It had a speed higher than that of any Chinese aircraft except the Soviet-supplied I-16.**

# Mitsubishi Ki-21 "Sally"

## Ki-21-I, -IIa and -IIb

**Origin:** Mitsubishi Jukogyo KK; also built by Nakajima Hikoki KK.
**Type:** Seven-seat heavy bomber.
**Engines:** (I) two 850hp Nakajima Ha-5-Kai 14-cylinder two-row radials; (II) two 1,490hp Mitsubishi Ha-101 of same layout.
**Dimensions:** Span 73ft 9¾in (22·5m); length 52ft 6in (16·0m); height 15ft 11in (4·85m).
**Weights:** Empty (I) 10,341lb (4691kg); (II) 13,382lb (6070kg); maximum loaded (I) 16,517lb (7492kg); (II) 21,395lb (9710kg).
**Performance:** Maximum speed (I) 268mph (432km/h); (II) 297mph (478km/h); initial climb (I) 1,150ft (350m)/min; (II) 1,640ft (500m)/min; service ceiling (I) 28,220ft (8600m); (II) 32,800ft (10,000m); range with full bomb load (I) 1,678 miles (2700km); (II) 1,370 miles (2200km).
**Armament:** See text for defensive armament; internal bomb bay in fuselage for load of (I) 1,653lb (750kg) or (II) 2,205lb (1000kg).
**History:** First flight November 1936; service delivery 1937; first flight (Ki-21-II) mid-1940; final delivery September 1944.
**User:** Japan (Imperial Army).

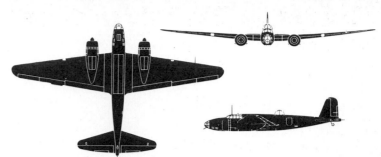

**Above: Three-view of the Ki-21-IIb.**

**Development:** In 1936 the Imperial Japanese Army issued a challenging specification for a new heavy bomber, demanding a crew of at least four, an endurance of five hours, a bomb load of 750kg and speed of 400km/h. Mitsubishi won over the Nakajima Ki-19 and built five prototypes powered by the company's own A.14 (Kinsei Ha-6) engine. The fields of fire of the three manually aimed 7·7mm machine guns were inadequate and the Army also requested a switch to the Ha-5 engine. With various modifications it was accepted as the Type 97 (also called OB-97; omoshi bakudanki meaning heavy bomber) and put into production not only by Mitsubishi but also, in 1938, by Nakajima. It rapidly became the premier Japanese Army heavy bomber and served throughout the "Chinese incident", the operational results being efficiently fed back to the procurement machine and the manufacturer. This led to the defensive armament being increased to five guns, one remotely controlled in the extreme tail, the crew being increased to seven. The bomb bay was enlarged, the flaps were increased in size and crew armour was dramatically augmented. The result was the Ki-21-Ib. Increase in fuel capacity and addition of a sixth (beam) gun resulted in the -Ic variant. In 1939 work began on the much more powerful -II, with increased-span tailplane. Several hundred of both versions were in use in December 1941 and they were met on all fronts in the Pacific war (being fairly easy meat for Hurricanes in Burma). Code-named "Sally" they faded from front-line service in 1943, though the -IIb with "glasshouse" replaced by a dorsal turret (one 12·7mm) improved defence when it entered service in 1942. Total production was 2,064 (351 by Nakajima), plus 500 transport versions (called MC-20, Ki-57 and "Topsy").

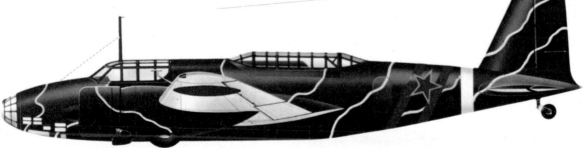

**Above: After the Japanese lost air supremacy the Ki-21 had to hug the trees to evade Allied fighters. This Ki-21-IIb belonged to the 14th Sentai (Group).**

**Left: Ki-21-Ia of the 2nd Chutai, 60th Hikosentai**

**Below: A formation of Ki-21-IIa bombers. The nearest bears markings of the Hammamatsu Bomber School.**

# Mitsubishi Ki-30 "Ann"

## Ki-30

**Origin:** Mitsubishi Jukogyo KK; also built by Tachikawa Dai-Ichi Rikugun Kokusho.
**Type:** Two-seat light bomber.
**Engine:** One 950hp Mitsubishi Ha-5 Zuisei 14-cylinder two-row radial.
**Dimensions:** Span 47ft 8¾in (14·55m); length 33ft 11in (10·34m); height 11ft 11¾in (3·65m).
**Weights:** Empty 4,915lb (2230kg); maximum loaded 7,324lb (3322kg).
**Performance:** Maximum speed 263mph (423km/h); initial climb 1,640ft (500m)/min; service ceiling 28,117ft (8570m); range (bomb load not stated) 1,056 miles (1700km).
**Armament:** One 7·7mm Type 89 machine gun fixed in wing (sometimes both wings) and one manually aimed from rear cockpit; internal bomb bay for three 220lb (100kg) or equivalent bomb load.
**History:** First flight February 1937; service delivery October 1938; final delivery 1941.

**Users:** Japan (Imperial Army), Thailand.

**Development:** With the Ki-32, Ki-27 fighter and Ki-21 heavy bomber, the Ki-30 was one of the important new stressed-skin monoplanes ordered by the Imperial Army under its modernisation plan of 1935. It was the first in Japan to have a modern two-row engine, as well as internal bomb bay, flaps and constant-speed propeller. It was notably smaller than the otherwise similar Fairey Battle produced in Britain. Unlike the British bomber the bomb bay was in the fuselage, resulting in a mid-wing and long landing gear (which was fixed). The pilot and observer/bomb aimer had a good view but were unable to communicate except by speaking tube. The Ki-30 was in service in numbers in time to be one of the major types in the Sino-Japanese war. In 1942 surviving aircraft played a large part in the advance to the Philippines, but then swiftly withdrew from first-line operations. Mitsubishi built 638 at Nagoya and 68 were completed at the Tachikawa Army Air Arsenal. In conformity with the Allied system of code-naming bombers after girls, the Ki-30 was dubbed "Ann". It was the ultimate development of the Karigane family of high-performance monoplanes.

**Left: A Ki-30 light attack bomber of the 2nd Chutai (Squadron or Company) of the 10th Hikosentai (Group). The Ki-30 saw most of its action on the Asian mainland.**

**Right: Pilots and observers of a Ki-30 Chutai relax before a mission, probably in China in 1938. Like other Imperial Army aircraft of the period these bombers are either grey or in natural metal finish. Escorted on their short-range missions by Ki-27 fighters, the losses of Ki-30 units were at first commendably low.**

# Mitsubishi Ki-46 "Dinah"

## Type 100 Models 1-4 (Ki-46-I to Ki-46-IVb)

**Origin:** Mitsubishi Jukogyo KK.
**Type:** Strategic reconnaissance (Ki-46-III-Kai, night fighter).
**Engines:** (I) two 870hp Mitsubishi Ha-26-I 14-cylinder two-row radials; (II) two 1,080hp Mitsubishi Ha-102 of same layout; (III) two 1,500hp Mitsubishi Ha-112-II of same layout; (IV) Ha-112-IIRu, same rated power but turbocharged.
**Dimensions:** Span 48ft 2¾in (14·7m); length (all except III-Kai) 36ft 1in (11·0m); (III-Kai) 37ft 8in (11·47m); height 12ft 8¾in (3·88m).
**Weights:** Empty (I) 7,450lb (3379kg); (II) 7,193lb (3263kg); (III) 8,446lb (3831kg); (IV) 8,840lb (4010kg); loaded (no overload permitted) (I) 10,630lb (4822kg); (II) 11,133lb (5050kg); (III) 12,620lb (5724kg); (IV) 13,007lb (5900kg); (III-Kai) 13,730lb (6227kg).
**Performance:** Maximum speed (I) 336mph (540km/h); (II) 375mph (604km/h); (III, III-Kai, IV) 391mph (630km/h); initial climb (I, II, III) about 1,970ft (600m)/min; (IV) 2,625ft (800m)/min; service ceiling (I, II, III) 34,500–36,000ft (10,500–11,000m); (IV) 38,000ft (11,500m); range (I) 1,305 miles (2100km); (II) 1,490 miles (2400km); (III) 2,485 miles (4000km); (III-Kai) 1,243 miles (2000km); (IV) not known, but at least 4000km.
**Armament:** (I, II) one 7·7mm manually aimed from rear cockpit; other types, none, except III-Kai, two 20mm Ho-5 cannon fixed in nose firing ahead and 37mm Ho-203 firing at elevation of 30° from top of fuselage.
**History:** First flight November 1939; (production II) March 1941; (III) December 1942; (III-Kai conversion) about September 1944.
**User:** Japan (Imperial Army).

**Development:** One of the most trouble-free and popular aircraft of the whole Pacific war, the Ki-46 "Shitei" (reconnaissance for HQ), code-named "Dinah" by the Allies, was one of only very few Japanese aircraft that could penetrate Allied airspace with some assurance it would survive. It was

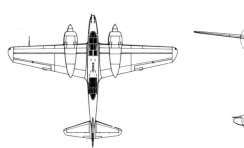

**Above: Three-view of Ki-46-III-Kai.**

also almost the only machine with the proven ability to operate at the flight levels of the B-29. In the first year of its use, which extended to every part of the Japanese war throughout the Pacific and China, much trouble was experienced from sparking-plug erosion and crew anoxia, both rectified by improved design and greater oxygen storage. Allied radar forced the Ki-46 to fly even faster and higher, leading to the almost perfectly streamlined Ki-46-III. These entered service in 1943, in which year many earlier versions were converted to Ki-46-II-Kai dual conversion trainers. Total production amounted to 1,742, all made by Mitsubishi at Nagoya and Toyama. Only four prototypes were finished of the turbocharged IVa, but many III models were hastily converted by the Army Tachikawa base into III-Kai night-fighters capable of intercepting B-29s. No radar was carried. At VJ-day Mitsubishi was trying to produce IIIc and IVb fighters and the IIIb ground-attack version.

**Right: Action shot of an attack by Allied aircraft on a Japanese airstrip in the south-west Pacific. Parachute-retarded bombs have just missed three Ki-46-II.**

**Below: A Ki-46-II of the 18th Independent Reconnaissance Chutai (Dokuritsu Dai Shijugo Chutai).**

# Mitsubishi Ki-67 Hiryu "Peggy"

## Ki-67-Ia, Ib and II and Ki-109

**Origin:** Mitsubishi Jukogyo KK; also built by Kawasaki and (assembly only) Nippon Kokusai Koku Kogyo KK, plus one by Tachikawa.

**Type:** Heavy bomber and torpedo dropper; Ki-109 heavy escort fighter.

**Engines:** Two 1,900hp Mitsubishi Ha-104 18-cylinder two-row radials.

**Dimensions:** Span 73ft 9¾in (22·5m); length 61ft 4¼in (18·7m); height 18ft 4½in (5·60m).

**Weights:** (lb) empty 19,068lb (8649kg); loaded 30,346lb (13,765kg).

**Performance:** (lb) Maximum speed 334mph (537km/h); initial climb 1,476ft (450m)/min; service ceiling 31,070ft (9470m); range with full bomb load 621 miles (1000km) plus 2hr reserve, also reported as total range 1,740 miles (2800km).

**Armament:** Standard on Ia, Ib, one 20mm Ho-5 in electric dorsal turret and single 12·7mm Type 1 manually aimed from nose, tail and two beam positions; internal bomb load 1,764lb (800kg); suicide attack 6,393lb (2900kg).

**History:** First flight "beginning of 1943"; service delivery April 1944; first flight (Ki-109) August 1944.

**User:** Japan (Imperial Army and Navy).

**Development:** Designed by a team led by Dr Hisanojo Ozawa to meet a February 1941 specification, this Army bomber not only met the demand for much higher speed but also proved to have the manoeuvrability of a fighter. It also lacked nothing in armour and fuel-tank protection, and was probably the best all-round bomber produced in Japan during World War II. With a crew of six/eight, it was often looped and shown to have excellent turning power, better than that of several Japanese fighters. Indeed the Ki-69 escort fighter version was developed in parallel with the bomber during 1942 but had to be shelved as delays to the bomber were becoming serious. These delays were due to inefficiency, material shortage and continual changes requested by the customer. By 1944 only 15 (all different) had been built, but production was then allowed to begin in earnest and by VJ-day the creditable total of 727 had been delivered, 606 by Mitsubishi and the rest by Kawasaki, Nippon and (one only) the Tachikawa arsenal. At first the Ki-67 Hiryu (Flying Dragon) was used as a torpedo bomber in the Philippine Sea battle, receiving the Allied name "Peggy". Later it operated against Iwo Jima, the Marianas and Okinawa and in the defence of Japan.

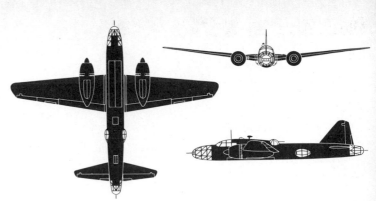

**Above: Three-view of Ki-67-Ib.**

There were only two versions used, the Ib having bulged waist blisters. Of many projected versions, of which the Ki-67-II with 2,500hp Ha-214 engines marked the biggest advance, only the Ki-109 reached the service trials stage. Armed with a 75mm gun with 15 hand-loaded rounds, plus a 12·7mm in the tail, this was meant to have 2,000hp turbocharged Ha-104 engines but none were available. With ordinary Ha-104s the Ki-109 could not get up to B-29 altitude!

**Below: Air-to-air photograph of a Ki-67-Ib of the 3rd Chutai of the 98th Sentai of the Imperial Army.**

**Left: Side elevation of a Ki-67-Ib of the Army's 74th Sentai. Colour was deep olive and pale grey.**

**Below: Though unit markings are not in evidence, this Ki-67-Ib is in full combat service. The Army loved it.**

# Nakajima B5N "Kate"

## B5N1 and B5N2

**Origin:** Nakajima Hikoki KK; also built by Aichi Tokei Denki and Dai-Juichi Kaigun Kokusho (Hiro).
**Type:** (B5N1) three-seat carrier-based bomber; (2) torpedo bomber.
**Engine:** (B5N1 Model 11) one 770hp Nakajima Hikari 3 nine-cylinder radial; (B5N1 Model 12) 970 or 985hp Nakajima Sakae 11 14-cylinder two-row radial; (B5N2) 1,115hp Sakae 21.
**Dimensions:** Span 50ft 11in (15·52m); length (1) 33ft 11in; (2) 33ft 9½in (10·3m); height 12ft 1¾in (3·70m).
**Weights:** Empty (1) 4,645lb (2107kg); (2) 5,024lb (2279kg); normal loaded (1) 8,047lb (3650kg); (2) 8,378lb (3800kg); maximum loaded (2) 9,039lb (4100kg).
**Performance:** Maximum speed (1) 217mph (350km/h); (2) 235mph (378km/h); initial climb (both) 1,378ft (420m)/min; service ceiling (both) about 25,000ft (7640m); range (1) 683 miles (1100km); (2) normal gross, 609 miles (980km), overload (4100kg) 1,237 miles (1990km).
**Armament:** (1) one 7·7mm Type 89 manually aimed from rear cockpit; underwing racks for two 551lb (250kg) or six 132lb (60kg) bombs; (2) two 7·7mm manually aimed from rear cockpit; two 7·7mm fixed above forward fuselage; centreline rack for 1,764lb (800kg, 18in) torpedo or three 551lb bombs.
**History:** First flight January 1937; (production B5N1) later 1937; (B5N2) December 1939; final delivery, probably 1942.
**User:** Japan (Imperial Navy).

**Development:** Designed to meet a 1935 requirement, the B5N was judged ordinary and obsolescent in World War II, yet in its day it was advanced and bold. The Japanese keenly studied the stressed-skin aircraft of Northrop, Douglas and Clark, and swiftly copied new features. The B5N had not only a thoroughly modern structure but also variable-pitch propeller (not on RAF Hurricanes until mid-1940!), hydraulically retracting landing gear, Fowler flaps, NACA cowling, integral wing fuel tanks and, until judged troublesome, hydraulic wing-folding. The challenging specification demanded a speed of 330km/h (205mph), but the prototype beat this by

**Right:** These are early B5N1 models, and the absence of certain operational features suggests that they are probably of the B5N1-K trainer version. Operational B5Ns were usually painted, upper surfaces often being dark green.

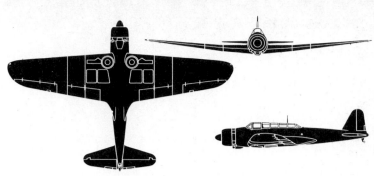

**Above: Three-view of B5N1 Model 11.**

23mph. The B5N1 went into production in time to serve in the Sino-Japanese war; a few of the rival fixed-gear Mitsubishi B5M were bought as an insurance. By 1940 some attack B5N were converted into B5N1-K trainers, but 103 bombed at Pearl Harbor. In the same attack 40 of the new B5N2 torpedo bombers took part, at least half finding their mark. Subsequently the B5N2 played the chief role in sinking the US carriers *Yorktown*, *Lexington*, *Wasp* and *Hornet*. They soldiered on into 1944 alongside their replacement the B6N. Total production was 1,149, including 200 by Aichi and 280 by Hiro Arsenal. Their Allied name was "Kate".

# Nakajima B6N Tenzan "Jill"

## B6N1, B6N2

**Origin:** Nakajima Hikoki KK.
**Type:** Three-seat carrier-based torpedo bomber.
**Engine:** (B6N1) one 1,870hp Nakajima Mamori 11 14-cylinder two-row radial; (B6N2) 1,850hp Mitsubishi Kasei 25 of same layout.
**Dimensions:** Span 48ft 10¼in (14·894m); length 35ft 7½in (10·865m); height (1) 12ft 1¾in (3·7m); (2) 12ft 5½in (3·8m).
**Weights:** Empty 6,636lb (3010kg) (1, 2 almost identical); normal loaded 11,464lb (5200kg); maximum overload 12,456lb (5650kg).
**Performance:** Maximum speed (1) 289mph (465km/h); (2) 299mph (482km/h); initial climb (1) 1,720ft (525m)/min; (2) 1,885ft (575m)/min; service ceiling (1) 28,379ft (8650m); (2) 29,659ft (9040m); range (normal weight) (1) 907 miles (1460km); (2) 1,084 miles (1745km), (overload) (1) 2,312 miles (3720km); (2) 1,895 miles (3050km).
**Armament:** One 7·7mm Type 89 manually aimed from rear cockpit and one manually aimed by middle crew-member from rear ventral position, with fixed 7·7mm firing forward in left wing (often absent from B6N1); 1,764lb

**Below:** A formation of Nakajima B6N2 torpedo bombers, probably photographed by the radio-operator/gunner of another. Colours are dark green and pale grey, with black engine cowls.

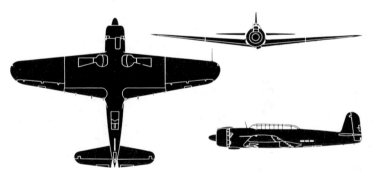

**Above: Three-view of B6N2, without radar.**

(800kg, 18in) torpedo carried offset to right of centreline, or six 220lb (100kg) bombs under fuselage.
**History:** First flight March 1942; service delivery (B6N1) early 1943; (B6N2) December 1943.
**User:** Japan (Imperial Navy).

**Development:** Named Tenzan (Heavenly Mountain) after a worshipped mountain in China, and code-named "Jill" by the Allies, the B6N was another conventional-looking aircraft which in fact was in many respects superior to the seemingly more advanced machines of the Allies (in this case the Grumman TBF and Fairey Barracuda). Designed as a replacement for B5N, Tenzan was slim and clean, with no internal weapon bay. The torpedo was offset, and to increase clearance on torpedo release the big oil cooler was offset in the other direction (to the left). The distinctive shape of the vertical tail was to minimise stowage length in the three-point attitude in carriers. Nakajima's big Mamori engine, driving a four-blade Hamilton-type propeller, suffered severe vibration and overheating, and though the B6N1 was kept in service it was replaced in production by the B6N2. The lower power of the proven Kasei was counteracted by the improved installation with less drag, and jet-thrust from the exhaust stubs. Tenzans went into action off Bougainville in the Marshalls campaign in June 1944. Subsequently they were heavily committed, many being later equipped with ASV radar for night attacks and ending in April-June 1945 with a hectic campaign of torpedo and suicide attacks off Okinawa and Kyushu. By this time the Imperial Navy had no operating carrier and hardly any skilled pilots.

47

# Nakajima C6N Saiun "Myrt"

## C6N1, 1-B and 1-S Saiun (Painted Cloud) (Allied code-name "Myrt")

**Origin:** Nakajima Hikoki KK, Koizuma and Haneda.
**Type:** Carrier-based strategic reconnaissance aircraft, (1-B) attack, (1-S) land-based night fighter.
**Engine:** 1,990hp Nakajima NK9H Homare 21 18-cylinder radial.
**Dimensions:** Span 41ft 0in (12·50m); length 36ft 1in (11·00m); height 13ft 0in (3·96m).
**Weights:** Empty 6,411lb (2908kg); loaded 9,921lb (4500kg); max overload 11,627lb (5274kg).
**Performance:** Maximum speed 378mph (609km/h); service ceiling 35,238ft (10,740m); range 1,914 miles (3080km); max range with overload fuel 3,300 miles (5310km).
**Armament:** (C6N1) one 7·92mm Type 2 manually aimed from rear cockpit; (1-B) forward-firing cannon and 1,764lb (800kg) torpedo; (1-S) two 20mm Type 99 cannon fixed obliquely in fuselage.
**History:** First flight 15 May 1943; service delivery July 1944; final delivery August 1945.
**User:** Japan (Imperial Navy).

**Development:** This outstandingly clean aircraft was an example of Japanese specialization defeated by circumstances. No other nation built a purpose-designed carrier-based reconnaissance aircraft in World War II, and the 17-Shi (spring 1942) specification was very challenging. The C6N was faintly like a Fw 190 stretched to seat a pilot, navigator/observer

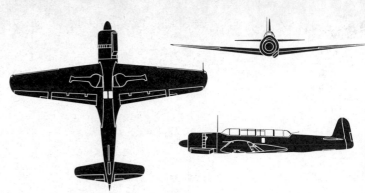

**Above: Three-view of C6N1, showing tabbed Fowler flaps and ventral observation/camera windows.**

and radio operator/gunner in tandem. As evidence of advanced design, the flaps were tabbed Fowlers, and the laminar-section wing (only slightly larger than a Zero's) also had drooping ailerons and slats, and was almost entirely given over to six integral tanks. The troublesome Homare was beautifully cowled and had thrust-giving ejector exhausts. Another feature that was new to Japan was thick-skinned structure, reducing the numbers of parts and cutting the number of rivets from 220,000 for a Zero to under 100,000. Altogether 463 of these speedy machines were built, but need for the C6N1-B was swept away by loss of the carrier force. Some Saiuns were converted as C6N1-S night fighters with crew of two and oblique cannon. There were many advanced prototypes and projected versions.

# Nakajima J1N1 "Irving"

## J1N1-C, J1N1-F, J1N1-S Gekko and J1N1-C-Kai

**Origin:** Nakajima Hikoki KK.
**Type:** (C, F) three-seat reconnaissance; (S, C-Kai) two-seat night fighter.
**Engines:** All operational versions, two 1,130hp Nakajima Sakae 21 14-cylinder two-row radials.
**Dimensions:** Span 55ft 8½in (16·98m); length (all, excluding nose guns or radar) 39ft 11½in (12·18m); height 14ft 11½in (4·562m).
**Weights:** Empty (C, S) 10,697lb (4852kg); loaded (C) 15,984lb (7250kg); (S) 15,212lb (6900kg); maximum overload (both) 16,594lb (7527kg).
**Performance:** Maximum speed (C, S) 315mph (507km/h); initial climb (C, S) 1,968ft (600m)/min; service ceiling 30,578ft (9320m); range (C, S, normal gross) 1,585 miles (2550km), (overload) 2,330 miles (3750km).
**Armament:** (J1N1-C) one 20mm Type 99 cannon and two 7·7mm Type 97 fixed in nose; (J1N1-S) four 20mm Type 99 Model 2 cannon fixed in rear cockpit, two firing obliquely upwards and two firing obliquely downwards; (J1N1-F) manual dorsal turret with single 20mm gun.
**History:** First flight May 1941; (production C) August 1942; service delivery (C) end of 1942; first flight (S) August 1943.
**User:** Japan (Imperial Navy).

**Development:** In 1938, before the Zero-Sen had flown, the Imperial Navy issued a specification for a twin-engined, long-range escort fighter, to reach a speed of 280 knots, and have a range of 1,300 nautical miles or 2,000 n.m. with extra fuel (the n.m. was the standard naval unit in Japan). Mitsubishi abandoned this project, but Nakajima's design team under K. Nakamura succeeded in producing a large prototype which proved to have remarkable manoeuvrability. Fitted with large fabric-covered ailerons, slotted flaps (opened 15° for combat) and leading-edge slats, it could dog-fight well with a Zero and the prototype was eventually developed to have

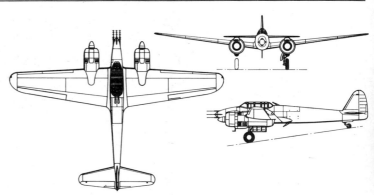

**Above: Three-view of J1N1-S Gekko night fighter.**

no flight limitations. But the Navy doubted the practicability of the complex scheme of two dorsal barbettes, each mounting two 7·7mm guns, remotely aimed in unison by the navigator. Eventually the Navy decided to buy the J1N1-C with these barbettes removed to serve as a three-seat photographic aircraft. (Some reports claim the failure as a fighter was due to lateral control problems, but Nakajima test pilots insist it was simply a matter of armament.) Soon after sorties began over the Solomons in the spring of 1943 the commander of the 251st Air Corps, Yasuna Kozono, hit on a way of intercepting Allied heavy night bombers. He had several aircraft modified as C-Kai night fighters with upper and lower pairs of oblique cannon. The armament proved effective, and most of the 477 J1N aircraft were built as J1N1-S Gekko (Moonlight) fighters with nose radar and a smoother cabin outline. They were good, robust aircraft, but unable to intercept the fast, high-flying B-29. Their Allied name was "Irving".

**Below: The first prototype of the J1N1-C, the production version of the original reconnaissance aircraft.**

# Nakajima Ki-27 "Nate"

## Ki-27a and -27b

**Origin:** Nakajima Hikoki KK; also built by Mansyu Hikoki Seizo KK.
**Type:** Single-seat interceptor fighter and light attack.
**Engine:** Prototype, one 650hp Nakajima Ha-1a (Jupiter-derived) nine-cylinder radial; 27a and 27b, one 710hp Ha-1b.
**Dimensions:** Span 37ft 0¾in (11·3m); length 24ft 8½in (7·53m); height 9ft 2¼in (2·8m).
**Weights:** Empty 2,403lb (1090kg); loaded 3,638lb (1650kg); (27b) up to 3,946lb.
**Performance:** Maximum speed 286mph (460km/h); initial climb 2,953ft (900m)/min; service ceiling, not recorded but about 34,400ft (10,500m); range 389 miles (625km).
**Armament:** Two 7·7mm Type 89 machine guns fixed in sides of fuselage, firing inside cowling; external racks for four 55lb (25kg) bombs.
**History:** First flight 15 October 1936; service delivery, early 1938; service delivery (Ki-27b) March 1939; final delivery July 1940.
**User:** Japan (Imperial Army) and Manchukuo.

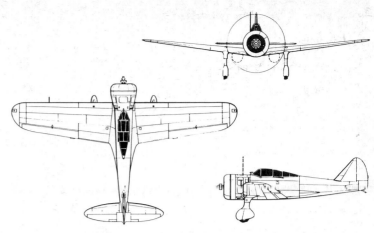

**Above: Three-view of the Ki-27b.**

**Development:** The Imperial Japanese Army's first low-wing monoplane fighter, the Ki-27 was in continuous production from 1937 to 1940 and was not only built in much larger quantities than other Japanese aircraft of its day but outnumbered almost every Japanese warplane of World War II. It was designed to meet a 1935 fighter requirement and competed against designs from Kawasaki and Mitsubishi. Though not the fastest, it was easily the most manoeuvrable; in fact it was probably the most manoeuvrable military aircraft of its day and possibly in all history, with plenty of engine power and (the Army having chosen the biggest of three possible sizes of wing) the extremely low loading of 17·9lb/ft². The loaded weight was roughly half that of contemporary Western fighters, and the penalty was paid in light construction and light armament. At the time Japanese pilots cared nothing for speed, fire-power or armour, but sacrificed everything for good visibility and manoeuvrability, and they resisted the introduction of later aircraft such as the Ki-43. Hundreds of Ki-27s fought Chinese and Soviet aircraft over Asia, scoring about 90 per cent of the claimed 1,252 Soviet aircraft (an exaggerated figure) shot down in 1939 after the Nomonhan Incident. Other Ki-27s served with the Manchurian air force, and at the time of Pearl Harbor they outnumbered all other Japanese fighters. Called "Nate" by the Allies, they continued in front-line use throughout the first year of the Pacific War. No fewer than 3,399 were built, 1,379 by the Manchurian (Mansyu Hikoki) company.

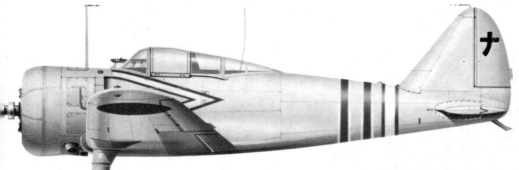

**Above: The Ki-27 was one of the most manoeuvrable fighters of all time. These two Ki-27b models bear on their rudders the badge of the Akeno Fighter Training School. Most World War II Army fighter pilots trained on Ki-27s.**

**Left: The colourful unit markings of this Ki-27b proclaim that it belongs to the 1st Chutai of the 1st Hikosentai, numerically the premier squadron of the Imperial Army.**

**Below: This early production Ki-27b — distinguished from the original Ki-27a model by the transparent glazing of the fairing behind the sliding main canopy, and various other details — was pictured in China in 1938-39. Hinomarus are seen on the wings apparently modified by transverse stripes, while a patriotic slogan adorns the fuselage.**

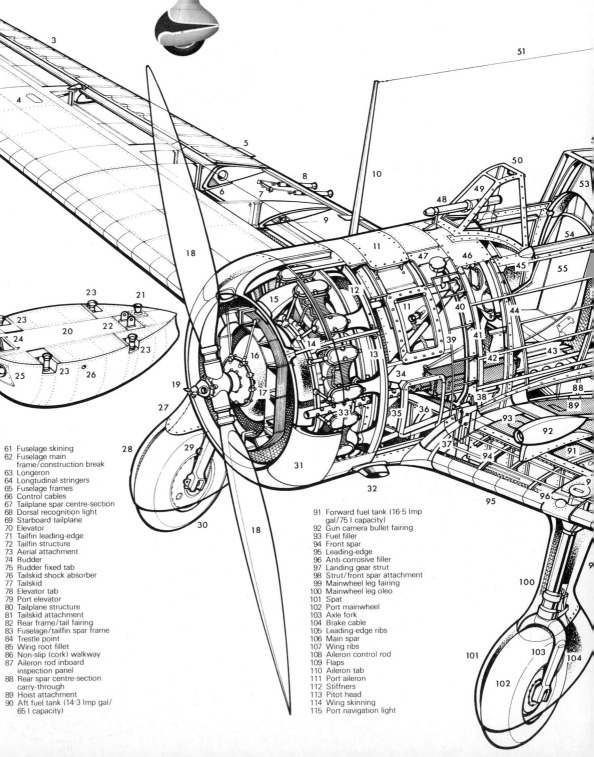

Left: Ki-27b in green for service in Burma with the 1st Chutai, 50th Sentai, in early 1942. Although popular with the Japanese pilots, the type was outmoded by the time of the Pacific war, at the start of which the Ki-27 outnumbered all other Japanese fighters.

Below: Ki-27b of the 3rd Chutai, 246th Sentai, based at Kakogawa for defence of the Osaka-Kobe region, early 1943.

**Nakajima Ki-27b cutaway drawing key**

1 Starboard navigation light
2 Wing skinning
3 Aileron
4 Aileron control rod inspection/access panel
5 Aileron fixed tab
6 Aileron nose balance weight
7 Flare igniter wire and release/drop cables
8 Magnesium flare illuminator tubes
9 Flap profile
10 Aerial mast
11 Access panels
12 Engine circumferential ring
13 Exhaust collector ring
14 650 hp Type 97 (Ha-1 otsu) radial engine
15 Carburettor air intakes
16 Support struts
17 Oil cooler assembly
18 Two-blade propeller
19 Starter dog
20 Auxiliary drop tank (attached starboard inner wing section)
21 Fuel pipe join
22 Aft attachment
23 Anti-swing fittings
24 Forward attachment
25 Fuel filler
26 Air vent
27 Mainwheel leg fairing
28 Starboard mainwheel spat
29 Axle fork
30 Starboard mainwheel
31 Nose ring
32 Exhaust
33 7.7-mm Type 89 machine gun
34 Engine bearers
35 Ammunition magazine
36 Cartridge ejector chute
37 Wing spar/fuselage forward attachment
38 Engine bearer mounting
39 Cooling gills
40 Fuselage main frame/engine bearer upper mounting
41 Control column
42 Gun loading/inspection panels
43 Seat support
44 Canted frame
45 Canopy track stop
46 Instrument panel
47 Fuel filler
48 Telescopic sight
49 Windshield
50 Rear-view mirror (internal)
51 Aerial
52 Rearward-sliding canopy hood
53 Turnover/crash pylon
54 Cockpit sill
55 Pilot's seat
56 Canted frame
57 Radio installation
58 Radio inspection panel
59 Aerial lead-in
60 Canopy aft (fixed) glazing

61 Fuselage skinning
62 Fuselage main frame/construction break
63 Longeron
64 Longtudinal stringers
65 Fuselage frames
66 Control cables
67 Tailplane spar centre-section
68 Dorsal recognition light
69 Starboard tailplane
70 Elevator
71 Tailfin leading-edge
72 Tailfin structure
73 Aerial attachment
74 Rudder
75 Rudder fixed tab
76 Tailskid shock absorber
77 Tailskid
78 Elevator tab
79 Port elevator
80 Tailplane structure
81 Tailskid attachment
82 Rear frame/tail fairing
83 Fuselage/tailfin spar frame
84 Trestle point
85 Wing root fillet
86 Non-slip (cork) walkway
87 Aileron rod inboard inspection panel
88 Rear spar centre-section carry-through
89 Hoist attachment
90 Aft fuel tank (14·3 Imp gal/65 l capacity)

91 Forward fuel tank (16·5 Imp gal/75 l capacity)
92 Gun camera bullet fairing
93 Fuel filler
94 Front spar
95 Leading-edge
96 Anti-corrosive filler
97 Landing gear strut
98 Strut/front spar attachment
99 Mainwheel leg fairing
100 Mainwheel leg oleo
101 Spat
102 Port mainwheel
103 Axle fork
104 Brake cable
105 Leading-edge ribs
106 Main spar
107 Wing ribs
108 Aileron control rod
109 Flaps
110 Aileron tab
111 Port aileron
112 Stiffners
113 Pitot head
114 Wing skinning
115 Port navigation light

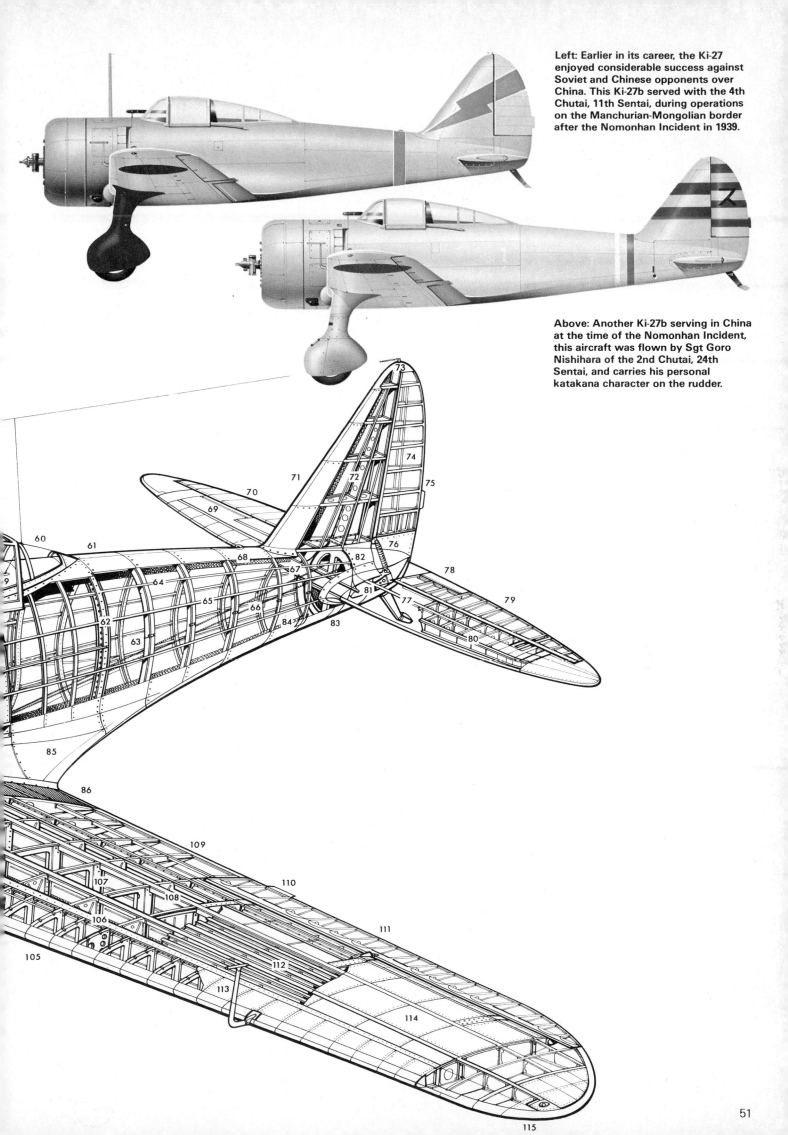

Left: Earlier in its career, the Ki-27 enjoyed considerable success against Soviet and Chinese opponents over China. This Ki-27b served with the 4th Chutai, 11th Sentai, during operations on the Manchurian-Mongolian border after the Nomonhan Incident in 1939.

Above: Another Ki-27b serving in China at the time of the Nomonhan Incident, this aircraft was flown by Sgt Goro Nishihara of the 2nd Chutai, 24th Sentai, and carries his personal katakana character on the rudder.

# Nakajima Ki-43 Hayabusa "Oscar"

## Ki-43-I to Ic, IIa and b, IIIa and b

**Origin:** Nakajima Hikoki KK; also built by Tachikawa Hikoki KK and Tachikawa Dai-Ichi Rikugun (Arsenal).

**Type:** Single-seat interceptor fighter (from IIa, fighter-bomber).

**Engine:** (Ki-43-I series) one 975hp Nakajima Ha-25 (Ha-35/12) Sakae 14-cylinder two-row radial; (II) 1,105hp Ha-115 Sakae; (III) 1,250hp Ha-112 (Ha-33/42) Kasei of same layout.

**Dimensions:** Span (I) 37ft 10½in; (IIa) 37ft 6¼in (11·437m); (IIb and subsequent) 35ft 6¾in (10·83m); length (I) 28ft 11¾in (8·82m); (II, III) 29ft 3¼in (8·92m); height (all) 10ft 8¾in (3·273m).

**Weights:** empty (I) 4,354lb (1975kg); normal loaded (I) 5,824lb (2642kg); (II series) 5,825–5,874lb (typically 2655kg); (III) 6,283lb (2850kg).

**Performance:** Maximum speed (I) 308mph; (II) 320mph (515km/h); (III) 363mph (585km/h); initial climb (typical II) 3,250ft (990m)/min; service ceiling (I) 38,500ft; (II, III) 36,800ft (11,215m); range (I) 746 miles (1200km); (II, III) internal fuel 1,060 miles (1700km), with two 45-gal drop tanks 1,864 miles (3000km).

**Armament:** (Ia) two 7·7mm Type 80 above engine; (Ib) one 12·7mm, one 7·7mm; (Ic) two 12·7mm; (all II series) two 12·7mm, each with 250 rounds, and wing racks for two 551lb (250kg) bombs; (IIIa) same; (IIIb) two 20mm Ho-5 cannon replacing 12·7mm in top decking, same bomb racks.

**History:** First flight January 1939; (production Ki-43-I) March 1941; (prototype IIa) February 1942; (prototype IIb) June 1942; (IIIa) December 1944.

**Users:** Japan (Imperial Army), Thailand; post-war, France (Indo-China) and Indonesia (against Dutch administration).

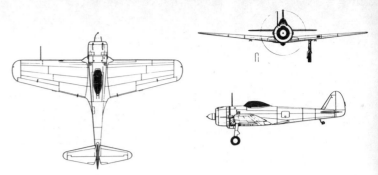

**Above: Three-view of the Ki-43-IIa.**

**Development:** Code-named "Oscar" by the Allies, the Ki-43 Hayabusa (Peregrine Falcon) was the most numerous of all Imperial Army warplanes and second only in numbers to the Zero-Sen. Compared with the famed Navy fighter it was smaller, lighter and much cheaper to produce. It was cast in the traditional Army mould in which everything was sacrificed for manoeuvrability, though the first prototype (designed by Hideo Itokawa to meet a 1938 Army contract which was simply awarded to Nakajima, without any industrial competition) was very heavy on the controls and disappointing. One prototype was even given fixed landing gear to save weight, but after many changes, and especially after adding a "combat manoeuvre flap" under the wings, the Ki-43 was turned into a dogfighter that could out-manoeuvre every aircraft ever ranged against it. After a few had carelessly got in the way of Allied fighters the more powerful II appeared with some armour, self-sealing tanks and slightly reduced span. The mass-produced clipped-wing IIb followed, serving in every Japanese battle. To the end,

**Nakajima Ki-43-I-Ko Hayabusa cutaway drawing key:**

1 Starboard navigation light
2 Wingtip
3 Starboard fabric-covered aileron
4 Aileron actuating linkage
5 Aileron control rod
6 Control rod connecting fittings
7 Aileron tab
8 Flap outer cable drum
9 Flap travel
10 Flap control cables
11 Radio mast
12 Light-alloy wing skinning
13 Starboard undercarriage fairing
14 Gun port fairings
15 Nose ring
16 Annular radiator/cooler
17 Two-blade two-pitch metal propeller
18 Spinner
19 Starter dog
20 Supercharger air intake
21 Intake fairing
22 Nakajima Ha-25 (Type 99) 14-cylinder two-row radial engine
23 Cowling gills
24 Exhaust collector ring
25 Exhaust outlet
26 Engine lower bearers
27 Oil regulator valve
28 Oil pressure tank
29 Engine accessories
30 Engine upper bearers
31 Cowling gill controls
32 Two 7.7-mm Type 89 machine guns
33 Gun gas outlet
34 Cartridge link ejection chute
35 Fireproof (No 1) bulkhead
36 Ammunition magazine (500 rpg)
37 Cartridge ejection chute
38 Gun breech fairing
39 Telescopic gun sight
40 One-piece curved windscreen
41 Radio aerial
42 Aft-sliding cockpit canopy
43 Turnover structure
44 Seat back
45 Seat adjustment rails
46 Seat pan
47 Throttle quadrant
48 Instrument panel
49 Control column

50 Rudder pedals
51 Underfloor control linkage
52 Seat support frame
53 Control cable and rod bearings
54 Oxygen cylinders
55 Rudder cable pulleys
56 Transceiver
57 Type 96 Hi-3 radio installation
58 Receiver unit
59 Transmitter unit
60 Anti-vibration mounting slings
61 Fuselage construction break
62 Inspection/access panel
63 Fuselage stringers
64 Fuselage structure
65 Frame
66 Fuselage upper longeron
67 Elevator control cables
68 Fuselage skinning
69 Tailwheel shock strut
70 Tail unit attachment
71 Tailfin root fairing

this nimble fighter remained totally deficient in firepower (except for the few examples of the IIb at the end of the war), and owing to its very light structure often disintegrated when hit by 0·5in fire. On the other hand, most of Japan's Army aces gained nearly all their scores on this popular little fighter. It was kept in production long after it was obsolete, 5,919 being delivered, including 2,629 by Tachikawa and 49 by the 1st Arsenal.

**Left: An interesting photograph of a Hayabusa, apparently a Ki-43-Ib, being refuelled from a bucket. Despite the Ki-44 Shoki in the background the aircraft is probably in Allied hands.**

**Below: This attractively painted Ki-43-IIa was assigned to the Imperial Army's 1st Chutai of the 50th Sentai, in mid-1943. The Ki-43 was, after the A6M Zero-Sen, the most numerous Japanese aircraft of World War II.**

**Above: The cutaway drawing shows the first production version of this trim fighter, the Ki-43-Ia (in Japanese, Ki-43-I-Ko). Outstandingly manoeuvrable, it was severely deficient in armament. Despite this, many Army aces gained most of their victories on the Ki-43, by accurate shooting – a quality shared by most of the top-scoring fighter pilots of all nations.**

72 Starboard tailplane
73 Elevator balance
74 Starboard elevator
75 Tailfin leading edge
76 Tailfin structure
77 Rear navigation light
78 Aerial attachment
79 Rudder upper hinge
80 Rudder post
81 Rudder frame
82 Rudder trim tab
83 Rudder middle hinge
84 Elevator control lever
85 Elevator trim tab

86 Elevator frame
87 Elevator balance
88 Tailplane structure
89 Rudder control lever
90 Non-retractable tailwheel
91 Cantilever tailwheel leg
92 Tailwheel leg/bulkhead attachment
93 Rudder cables
94 Fuselage skinning
95 Wing-root fairing
96 Flap inboard profiles
97 Flap actuating cylinder
98 Rear spar/fuselage attachment
99 Mainspar/fuselage attachment
100 Front spar/fuselage attachment
101 Port main fuel tank (29·5 Imp gal/132 litres capacity)
102 Port overload fuel tank (33 Imp gal/150 litres capacity)
103 Fuel filler caps
104 Main spar
105 Rear spar
106 Aileron control rod
107 Flap inboard travel
108 Flap pulley fairing
109 Fowler-type "butterfly" combat flap
110 Flap outboard travel
111 Aileron trim tab

112 Aileron inner hinge
113 Aileron centre hinge/ control rod attachment
114 Port aileron
115 Aileron outer hinge
116 Port wingtip
117 Port navigation light
118 Wing skinning
119 Pitot head
120 Leading edge ribs
121 Front spar
122 Landing light
123 Mainwheel leg fairing
124 Torque links
125 Port mainwheel
126 Axle fork
127 Mainwheel oleo
128 Mainwheel leg pivot
129 Gear support bearer
130 Gear actuating cylinder
131 Emergency actuation cables
132 Leading edge rib cut-outs
133 Mainwheel well
134 Underwing drop tank pylon (mounted aft and just inboard of the main undercarriage attachment point)
135 Tank suspension lugs
136 Air vent
137 Fuel pipe connection
138 Tank fin
139 Sway brace attachment points
140 Jettisonable 44 Imp gal (200 litres) tank

# Nakajima Ki-44 Shoki "Tojo"

## Ki-44-Ia, b and c, IIa, b and c and III

**Origin:** Nakajima Hikoki KK.
**Type:** Single-seat interceptor fighter and (II onwards) fighter-bomber.
**Engine:** (Ia) one 1,260hp Nakajima Ha-41 14-cylinder two-row radial; (Ib and all subsequent) 1,520hp Nakajima Ha-109 of same layout.
**Dimensions:** Span 31ft (9·448m); length 28ft 8½in (8·75m); height 10ft 8in (3·248m).
**Weights:** Empty (Ia) 3,968lb (1800kg); (II, typical) 4,643lb (2106kg); normal loaded (no overload permitted) (Ia) 5,622lb (2550kg); (IIc) 6,107lb (2770kg); (III) 5,357lb (2430kg).
**Performance:** Maximum speed (Ia) 360mph (579km/h); (IIc) 376mph (605km/h); initial climb (IIc) 3,940ft (1200m)/min; service ceiling (IIc) 36,745ft (11,200m); range on internal fuel (typical) 560 miles (900km) (endurance, 2hr 20min).
**Armament:** (Ia) two 12·7mm Type I in wings and two 7·7mm Type 89 in fuselage; (Ib, IIa, IIb) four 12·7mm Type I, two in fuselage and two in wings, with (II series) wing racks for two 220lb (100kg) bombs; (IIc) two 12·7mm in fuselage, two 40mm Ho-301 low-velocity cannon; (III) two 12·7mm in

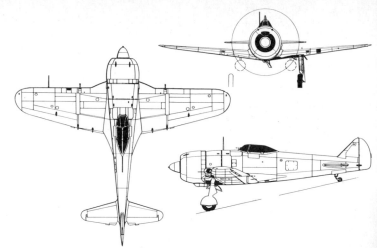

**Above: Three-view of Ki-44-IIb.**

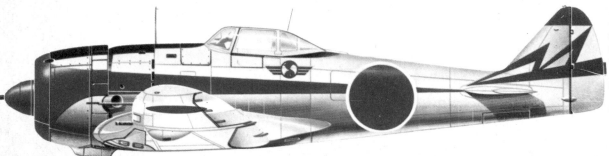

**Left: A mainly unpainted Ki-44-IIb of the Shinten (Sky Shadow) experimental unit of the 47th Sentai, based at Narimasu, Tokyo, in summer of 1944.**

**Right: A Ki-44-Ic, the rare interim model of late 1942. Only 40 were built of all Dash-I models combined.**

# Nakajima Ki-49 Donryu "Helen"

## Ki-49-I, IIa, IIb, III and Ki-58

**Origin:** Nakajima Hikoki KK; also built by Tachikawa Hikoki KK and (few) Mansyu Hikoki.
**Type:** Eight-seat heavy bomber; Ki-58, escort fighter.
**Engines:** (I) two 1,250hp Nakajima Ha-41 14-cylinder two-row radials; (II) two 1,450hp Nakajima Ha-109-II of same layout; (III) two 2,500hp Nakajima Ha-117 18-cylinder two-row radials.
**Dimensions:** Span 66ft 7¼in (20·3m); length 53ft 1¾in (16·2m); height 13ft 11½in (4·25m).
**Weights:** Empty (II) 15,653lb (7100kg); normal loaded 23,545lb

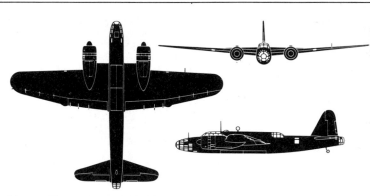

**Above: Three-view of Ki-49-I (II has oil coolers under engines).**

**Above: Take-off by one of the few (129) Ki-49-I production aircraft. This example bears on its tail the badge of the Hammamatsu Heavy Bomber Training School (also see page 155).**

**Below: Side elevation of a Ki-49-IIb, of an unknown sentai operating in New Guinea in late 1943.**

(10,680kg).
**Performance:** Maximum speed (II) 304mph (490km/h); initial climb 1,312ft (400m)/min; service ceiling 26,772ft (8160m); range with bomb load, 1,491 miles (2400km).
**Armament:** (I) one 20mm cannon manually aimed in dorsal position, single 7·7mm manually aimed at nose and tail; (IIa) as (I) plus extra 7·7mm in ventral and two beam positions (total five); (IIb) as IIa but with all 7·7mm replaced by 12·7mm, thus 20mm dorsal and single 12·7mm in nose, tail, ventral and two beam positions; all versions, internal bay for bomb load up to 2,205lb (1,000kg).
**History:** First flight August 1939; (production Ki-49-I) probably May 1940; (II) 1942; final delivery December 1944.
**User:** Japan (Imperial Army).

**Development:** Designed to a late 1938 specification aimed at replacing the Mitsubishi Ki-21, the Ki-49 was the first Japanese bomber to mount a 20mm cannon; but it was at first only slightly faster than the Ki-21, had a

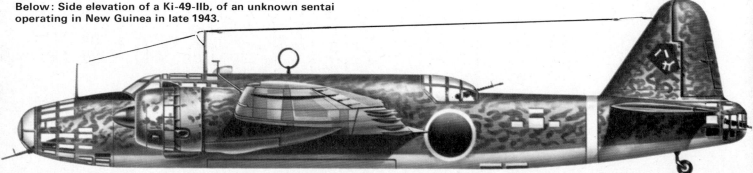

fuselage, two 20mm Ho-5 cannon in wings.

**History:** First flight (first of ten prototypes) August 1940; (production Ki-44-Ia) May 1942; (Ib, Ic) 1943; (IIb) December 1943.

**User:** Japan (Imperial Army).

**Development:** Marking a complete break with the traditional emphasis on manoeuvrability, the Ki-44 (code-named "Tojo" by the Allies) contrasted with the Ki-43 as did the J2M with the Zero-Sen. Suddenly the need was for greater speed and climb, even at the expense of poorer manoeuvrability and faster landing. In late 1940 a Ki-44 was tested against a Kawasaki Ki-60 and an imported Bf 109E, outflying both; but production was delayed until mid-1942 by the priority accorded the old Ki-43. Pilots did not like the speedy small-winged fighter, with poor view on take-off and such poor control that flick rolls and many other manoeuvres were banned. But gradually the fact that the Ki-44 could climb and dive as well as its enemies brought some measure of popularity, even though many inexperienced pilots were killed in accidents. Most Shokis (Demons) were -II series with retractable tailwheel and other changes, including a glazed teardrop canopy. The heavy cannon of the -IIc, firing caseless ammunition at 400 rounds per minute, were effective against Allied bombers. Probably the most successful mission ever flown in defending Japan was that of 19 February 1945 when a small force of Ki-44 (probably -IIc) climbed up to 120 B-29s and destroyed ten, two reportedly by suicide collisions. Total production was 1,233, including a few of the lightened -III series.

poor ceiling and never did achieve any advance in range and bomb load. The 1,160hp Nakajima Ha-5B engines of the prototype were replaced by the Ha-41, and 129 of the -I model were built at Ohta, after whose Donryu (Dragon Swallower) shrine the type was named. The production machine was the Type 100 heavy bomber, and the Allied code name was "Helen". Its first mission was a raid on Port Darwin from a New Guinea base on 19 February 1942. The main model was the better-armed -II series, of which 649 were built by Nakajima, 50 by Tachikawa and a few by Mansyu in Harbin, Manchuria. Though met in all parts of the Japanese war, the Ki-49 was not very effective; many were destroyed at Leyte Gulf, and by late 1944 all were being used either for non-combatant purposes or as suicide machines or, with ASV radar or magnetic-mine detectors, for ocean patrol. As it was a poor bomber three were converted as Ki-58 fighters with five 20mm cannon and three 12·7mm guns, while two were rebuilt as Ki-80 leadships for attack by fighter-bomber or suicide aircraft. The much more powerful III model was not ready by August 1945, though six were built.

**Below: This photograph is probably the best surviving of any type of Donryu. The subject is the mass-produced Ki-49-IIb, and the unit possibly the 110th Hikosentai.**

# Nakajima Ki-84 Hayate "Frank"

## Ki-84-I to Ic, and many projects

**Origin:** Nakajima Hikoki KK; also built by Mansyu Hikoki Seizo KK and (three Ki-106) Tachikawa Hikoki KK.
**Type:** Single-seat fighter-bomber.
**Engine:** In all production models, one 1,900hp Nakajima Homare Ha-45 Model 11 18-cylinder two-row radial.
**Dimensions:** Span 36ft 10½in (11·238m); length 32ft 6½in (9·92m); height 11ft 1¼in (3·385m).
**Weights:** Empty 5,864lb (2680kg); normal loaded 8,267lb (3750kg); maximum overload (seldom authorised) 9,150lb (4150kg).
**Performance:** Maximum speed 388mph (624km/h); initial climb 3,600ft (1100m)/min; service ceiling 34,450ft (10,500m); range on internal fuel 1,025 miles (1650km); range with 98-gal drop tanks, 1,815 miles (2920km).
**Armament:** (Ia) two 20mm Ho-5 in wings, each with 150 rounds, and two 12·7mm Type 103 in top of fuselage with 350 rounds; (Ib) four 20mm, each

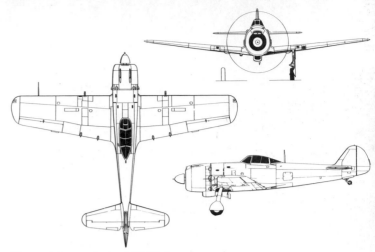

**Above: Three-view of Ki-84-Ia.**

**Left: Most Hayates were camouflaged or painted in various green shades. This pretty specimen served with HQ Chutai, 29th Sentai, on Taiwan (Formosa) in the summer of 1945.**

**Right: A more regular paint scheme is seen on this Ki-84-Ia of the 1st Chutai, 73rd Sentai, based in the Philippine Islands in December 1944.**

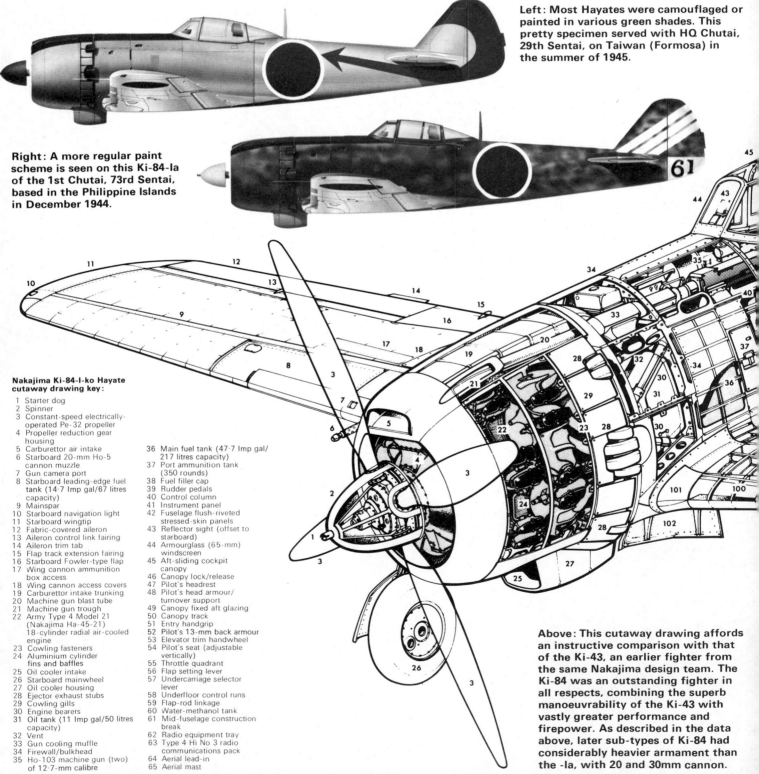

**Nakajima Ki-84-I-ko Hayate cutaway drawing key:**

1 Starter dog
2 Spinner
3 Constant-speed electrically-operated Pe-32 propeller
4 Propeller reduction gear housing
5 Carburettor air intake
6 Starboard 20-mm Ho-5 cannon muzzle
7 Gun camera port
8 Starboard leading-edge fuel tank (14·7 Imp gal/67 litres capacity)
9 Mainspar
10 Starboard navigation light
11 Starboard wingtip
12 Fabric-covered aileron
13 Aileron control link fairing
14 Aileron trim tab
15 Flap track extension fairing
16 Starboard Fowler-type flap
17 Wing cannon ammunition box access
18 Wing cannon access covers
19 Carburettor intake trunking
20 Machine gun blast tube
21 Machine gun trough
22 Army Type 4 Model 21 (Nakajima Ha-45-21) 18-cylinder radial air-cooled engine
23 Cowling fasteners
24 Aluminium cylinder fins and baffles
25 Oil cooler intake
26 Starboard mainwheel
27 Oil cooler housing
28 Ejector exhaust stubs
29 Cowling gills
30 Engine bearers
31 Oil tank (11 Imp gal/50 litres capacity)
32 Vent
33 Gun cooling muffle
34 Firewall/bulkhead
35 Ho-103 machine gun (two) of 12·7-mm calibre
36 Main fuel tank (47·7 Imp gal/217 litres capacity)
37 Port ammunition tank (350 rounds)
38 Fuel filler cap
39 Rudder pedals
40 Control column
41 Instrument panel
42 Fuselage flush-riveted stressed-skin panels
43 Reflector sight (offset to starboard)
44 Armourglass (65-mm) windscreen
45 Aft-sliding cockpit canopy
46 Canopy lock/release
47 Pilot's headrest
48 Pilot's head armour/turnover support
49 Canopy fixed aft glazing
50 Canopy track
51 Entry handgrip
52 Pilot's 13-mm back armour
53 Elevator trim handwheel
54 Pilot's seat (adjustable vertically)
55 Throttle quadrant
56 Flap setting lever
57 Undercarriage selector lever
58 Underfloor control runs
59 Flap-rod linkage
60 Water-methanol tank
61 Mid-fuselage construction break
62 Radio equipment tray
63 Type 4 Hi No 3 radio communications pack
64 Aerial lead-in
65 Aerial mast

**Above: This cutaway drawing affords an instructive comparison with that of the Ki-43, an earlier fighter from the same Nakajima design team. The Ki-84 was an outstanding fighter in all respects, combining the superb manoeuvrability of the Ki-43 with vastly greater performance and firepower. As described in the data above, later sub-types of Ki-84 had considerably heavier armament than the -Ia, with 20 and 30mm cannon.**

with 150 rounds, two in wings and two in fuselage; (Ic) two 20mm in fuselage and two 30mm Ho-105 cannon in wings; (all operational models) two racks under outer wings for tanks or bombs up to 551lb (250kg) each.
**History:** First flight March 1943; (production Ia) August 1943; service delivery April 1944.
**User:** Japan (Imperial Army).

**Left: An early Ki-84-Ia Hayate. The long landing gears were prone to structural failure, as a result of faulty heat-treatment of the steel legs, and the complex and closely cowled engine gave prolonged trouble; so did the hydraulics.**

**Below: The skull and crossbones insignia identify this Hayate, another Ki-84-Ia, as belonging to the 58th Shimbu-tai in Japan in August 1945.**

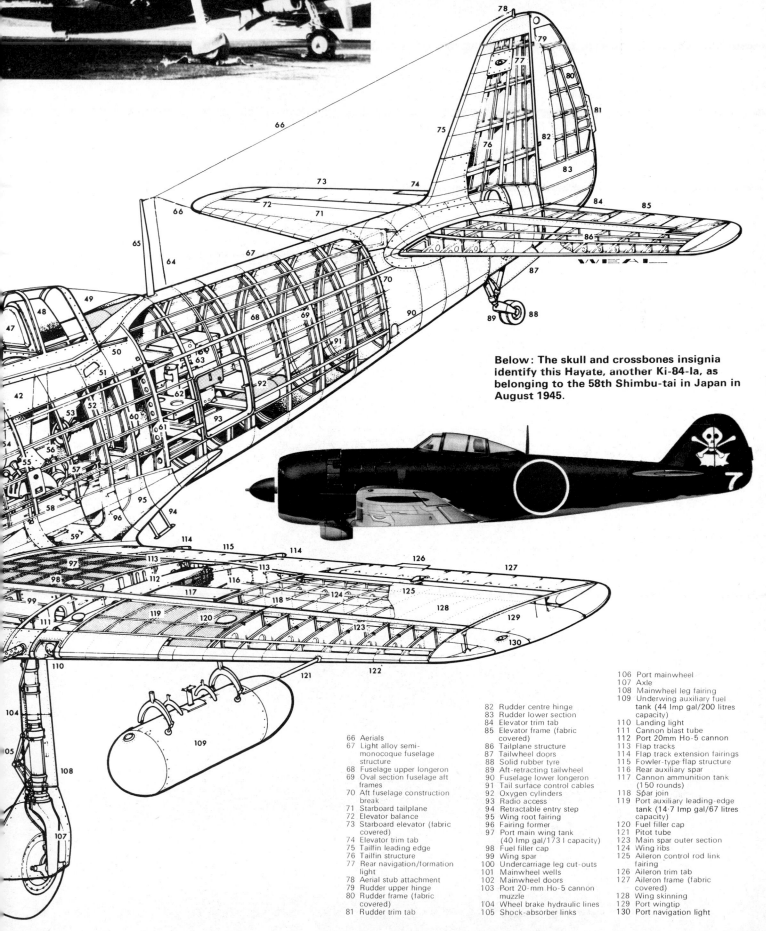

66 Aerials
67 Light alloy semi-monocoque fuselage structure
68 Fuselage upper longeron
69 Oval section fuselage aft frames
70 Aft fuselage construction break
71 Starboard tailplane
72 Elevator balance
73 Starboard elevator (fabric covered)
74 Elevator trim tab
75 Tailfin leading edge
76 Tailfin structure
77 Rear navigation/formation light
78 Aerial stub attachment
79 Rudder upper hinge
80 Rudder frame (fabric covered)
81 Rudder trim tab

82 Rudder centre hinge
83 Rudder lower section
84 Elevator trim tab
85 Elevator frame (fabric covered)
86 Tailplane structure
87 Tailwheel doors
88 Solid rubber tyre
89 Aft-retracting tailwheel
90 Fuselage lower longeron
91 Tail surface control cables
92 Oxygen cylinders
93 Radio access
94 Retractable entry step
95 Wing root fairing
96 Fairing former
97 Port main wing tank (40 Imp gal/173 l capacity)
98 Fuel filler cap
99 Wing spar
100 Undercarriage leg cut-outs
101 Mainwheel wells
102 Mainwheel doors
103 Port 20-mm Ho-5 cannon muzzle
104 Wheel brake hydraulic lines
105 Shock-absorber links

106 Port mainwheel
107 Axle
108 Mainwheel leg fairing
109 Underwing auxiliary fuel tank (44 Imp gal/200 litres capacity)
110 Landing light
111 Cannon blast tube
112 Port 20mm Ho-5 cannon
113 Flap tracks
114 Flap track extension fairings
115 Fowler-type flap structure
116 Rear auxiliary spar
117 Cannon ammunition tank (150 rounds)
118 Spar join
119 Port auxiliary leading-edge tank (14·7 Imp gal/67 litres capacity)
120 Fuel filler cap
121 Pitot tube
123 Main spar outer section
124 Wing ribs
125 Aileron control rod link fairing
126 Aileron trim tab
127 Aileron frame (fabric covered)
128 Wing skinning
129 Port wingtip
130 Port navigation light

► **Development:** Code-named "Frank" by the Allies, the Ki-84 of the Imperial Army was generally regarded as the best Japanese fighter of World War II. Yet it was not without its problems. Part of its fine all-round performance stemmed from the extremely advanced direct-injection engine, the first Army version of the Navy NK9A; yet this engine gave constant trouble and needed skilled maintenance. T. Koyama designed the Ki-84 to greater strength factors than any earlier Japanese warplane, yet poor heat-treatment of the high-strength steel meant that landing gears often simply snapped. Progressive deterioration in quality control meant that pilots never knew how particular aircraft would perform, whether the brakes would work or whether, in trying to intercept B-29s over Japan, they would even be able to climb high enough. Despite this, the Ki-84 was potentially superb, a captured -Ia out-climbing and outmanoeuvring a P-51H and P-47N! First batches went to China, where the 22nd Sentai flew rings round Gen Chennault's 14th Air Force. The unit then moved to the Philippines, where the rot set in, with accidents, shortages and extremely poor serviceability. Frequent bombing of the Musashi engine factory and extreme need to conserve raw material led to various projects and prototypes made of wood (Ki-84-II series and Ki-106) or steel (Ki-113) and advanced models with the 2,000hp Ha-45ru turbo charged engine, Ha-45/44 with two-stage three-speed blower and 2,500hp Ha-44/13. Total production of the Hayate (Hurricane) was 3,514 (2,689 at Ohta, 727 at Utsonomiya and 95 in Manchuria by Mansyu, which also flew the Ki-116 with smaller Ha-112 engine) and three at Tachikawa.

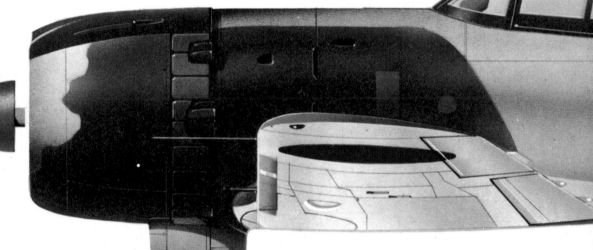

**Below: Yet another of the early Ki-84-Ia models, in this case belonging to the 11th Sentai in the south-west Pacific in mid-1944. Just beneath the trailing edge of the wing can be seen the combat manoeuvre flaps in the 'down' position.**

**Left: A Ki-84-Ia of the 1st Chutai, 47th Sentai, based at Narumatsu in August 1945. Markings may be compared with the 47th Sentai Ki-44.**

**Right: This Ki-84-Ia has the colourful tail marking of the 1st Chutai, 102nd Sentai, based at an airfield in Kyushu in April 1945.**

**Left: A shotai (section) from the 52nd Sentai about to leave on an attack mission. Each carries one drop tank (left) and a bomb (right).**

**Above: Many of the countless variations of Japanese military aircraft markings in World War II involved small or large areas of unpainted metal. This Ki-84-Ia of the 183rd Shimbu-tai, based at Tatebayashi, Japan, in August 1945, is a good example of roughly half-and-half. The Hinomaru on the fuselage has a narrow white outer ring, but many aircraft operating in the defence of Japan in 1945 had it on a broad white square or band.**

# Nakajima Ki-115 Tsurugi

### Ki-115 and various proposed developments (no Allied code-name published)

**Origin:** Designed by Aori Kunihiro assisted by Mitaka Research and Ota Manufacturing; prototype by Mitaki and production by Nakajima at Iwate and Ota.
**Type:** Single-seat suicide attack aircraft.
**Engine:** 1,150hp Nakajima Ha-35 Type 23 (Ha-115 Sakae) 14-cylinder radial.
**Dimensions:** Span 28ft 0½in (8·55m); length 28ft 2½in (8·60m); height 10ft 10in (3·30m).
**Weights:** Empty 3,616lb (1640kg); loaded 5,688lb (2580kg); max overload with 800kg bomb 6,349lb (2880kg).
**Performance:** Maximum speed 342mph (550km/h); range with 500kg bomb 746 miles (1200km).
**Armament:** Belly recess for bomb of 551lb (250kg), 1,102lb (500kg) or 1,764lb (800kg).
**History:** First flight March 1945.
**User:** Not delivered.

**Development:** As the concept of piloted suicide attacks had become firmly established during 1944 the Imperial Army recognised that it was inefficient to use a motley collection of unsuitable aircraft, and that an aircraft designed for such attack should be produced with extreme urgency. Nakajima was given the job on 20 January 1945, and the first aircraft emerged within three months. One might have expected the Ki-115 to be wooden, but instead the small wing was all-metal stressed-skin, the fuselage was steel tube with skin panels mainly of thin mild steel, and the tail was wood/fabric. The landing gear was unsprung steel tube, and arranged to be jettisoned after take-off. Handling was atrocious, but improved when a new sprung landing gear and bolted-on wing flaps were fitted. By VJ-day Nakajima had built 22 and the Ota plant 82, all with wing fixtures for rockets (never fitted) to boost speed in the final dive. The Ki-115b was a development with larger wings and all-wood structure and the Toka a proposed Navy version. The significantly more effective Ki-230 was not built.

**Right: The Ki-115 was possibly the cheapest manned combat aircraft of World War II, but it was also one of the least satisfactory. Few photographs exist of this hastily contrived and elusive machine, which, had it been started earlier, might have been a thorn in the side of the Allies. Unusually, this specimen appears to have a dark-painted fuselage.**

# Tachikawa Ki-36/ Ki-55 "Ida"

**Ki-36 (Army Type 98 Direct Co-operation),
Ki-55 (Army Type 99 trainer)
(Allied code-name "Ida")**

**Origin:** Tachikawa Hikoki KK, second-source production by Kawasaki.
**Type:** Ki-36, two-seat army co-operation; Ki-55, advanced trainer.
**Engine:** 510hp Hitachi Ha-13a (Army Type 98) nine-cylinder radial.
**Dimensions:** Span 38ft 8½in (11·80m); length 26ft 3in (8·00m); height 11ft 11¼in (3·64m).
**Weights:** Empty (36) 2,749lb (1247kg); loaded (36) 3,635lb (1649kg).

**Below: This Ki-36 "direct co-operation" aircraft could have been photographed on any front on which Japan fought from 1939 onwards. By 1943 most survivors were in China.**

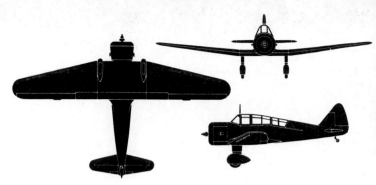

**Above: Three-view showing Ki-36 spats but no belly windows.**

**Performance:** Maximum speed (36) 217mph (349km/h); range 767 miles (1235km).
**Armament:** Synchronized 7·7mm Type 89 on right above fuselage (36 and 55), one Type 89 manually aimed from rear cockpit (36 only) and underwing racks for ten 27·5lb (12·5kg) or 33lb (15kg) bombs (36 only).
**History:** First flight (36) 20 April 1938; service delivery, early 1939; final delivery January 1944.
**Users:** Japan (Imperial Army), Manchukuo and Thailand (puppet states); post-war, Indonesia insurgent AF.

**Development:** Though little known, these were among the most common Japanese aircraft of the World War II period. The Ki-36 was designed to meet a May 1937 specification for an army co-operation machine able to use forward airstrips and carry cameras, radio and light anti-personnel bombs. Both pilot and observer had a good view, the latter having windows in the floor. Early service in China was extremely successful, but against the Allies casualties were heavy and from 1943 the type was withdrawn to secondary areas, though in late 1944 some appeared with 1,102lb (500kg) bombs in the suicide role. Total production was 1,334. The Ki-55 trainer was simpler, with no combat gear, spats or belly windows. It was the chief wartime advanced trainer of the Japanese and satellite air forces, 1,389 being built.

# Yokosuka D4Y Suisei "Judy"

**D4Y1 and 1-C, D4Y2, 2-C and 2-S,
D4Y3 and D4Y4**

**Origin:** Dai-Ichi Kaigun Koku Gijitsusho, Yokosuka; production aircraft built by Aichi Kokuki KK and Dai-Juichi Kaigun Kokusho.
**Type:** Two-seat carrier dive bomber; (1-C, 2-C, reconnaissance; 2-S night fighter; D4Y4, single-seat Kamikaze.
**Engines:** (1) one 1,200hp Aichi Atsuta 21 inverted-vee-12 liquid-cooled (Daimler-Benz 601); (2) 1,400hp Atsuta 32; (3, 4) 1,560hp Mitsubishi Kinsei 62 14-cylinder two-row radial).
**Dimensions:** Span (1, 2) 37ft 8½in (11·493m); (3, 4) 37ft 9in (11·50m); length (all, despite engine change) 33ft 6½in (10·22m); height (1, 2) 12ft 1in (3·67m); (3, 4) 12ft 3¼in (3·74m).
**Weights:** Empty (1) 5,650lb (2565kg); (2) 5,840lb (2635kg); (3) 5,512lb (2501kg); (4) variable; maximum loaded (1) 9,615lb (4361kg); (2) 9,957lb (4353kg); (3) 10,267lb (4657kg); (4) 10,434lb (4733kg).
**Performance:** Maximum speed (1) 339mph (546km/h); (2) 360mph (580km/h); (3) 356mph (574km/h); initial climb (1) 1,970ft (600m)/min; (others) 2,700ft (820m)/min; service ceiling (typical) 34,500ft (10,500m); range (2) 749 miles (1205km); (3) 945 miles (1520km).
**Armament:** Normally, two 7·7mm Type 97 fixed above engine, one 7·7mm manually aimed from rear cockpit; internal bomb bay for single 551lb (250kg) bomb, plus one 66lb (30kg) bomb under each wing; (4) see text.
**History:** First flight November 1940; (production D4Y1) May 1941; service delivery, late 1941.
**User:** Japan (Imperial Navy).

**Development:** Designed to a challenging specification of the Imperial Japanese Navy of 1937, which called for a long-range two-seat dive bomber as fast as the "Zero" fighter, the D4Y was one of the very few Japanese aircraft to go into production with a liquid-cooled engine. The supposed lower drag of such an engine had been one of the factors in meeting the requirement, but the Japanese version of the DB 601 had an unhappy history in carrier service. The first D4Y versions in combat were 1-C reconnaissance aircraft flying from the carrier *Soryu* during the Battle of Midway in June 1942. The carrier was sunk in that encounter, and soon most D4Y were being operated by unskilled crews from island airstrips. In 1943 the main problems with the aircraft — named Suisei (Comet), and called "Judy" by the Allies — were solved by switching to the smooth and reliable radial engine. During the final year of the war the D4Y4 appeared as a single-seat suicide attacker carrying 1,764lb (800kg) of explosives, while some dozens of Atsuta-engined examples were turned into 2-S night fighters with one or two 20mm cannon fixed obliquely behind the rear cockpit. Total production was 2,038.

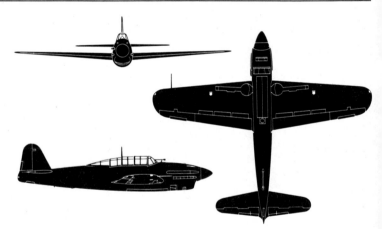

**Above: Three-view of D4Y1 (D4Y2 very similar).**

**Below: A D4Y3 Suisei Model 33, with two 72·6 Imp gal drop tanks. By the time this radial-engined model was delivered nearly all Suiseis had to be assigned to land-based units.**

# Yokosuka P1Y1 Ginga "Frances"

## P1Y1 Model 11, P1Y1-S, P1Y2 and 2-S

**Origin:** Design by Dai-Ichi Kaigun Koku Gijitsusho, but all construction by Nakajima Hikoki KK and Kawanishi Kokuki KK.
**Type:** Three-seat multi-role attack bomber; -S, two-seat night fighter.
**Engines:** (1) two 1,820hp Nakajima Ho-21 Homare 11 18-cylinder two-row radials; (2) 1,825hp Mitsubishi Kasei 25 14-cylinder two-row radials.
**Dimensions:** Span 65ft 7½in (20m); length 49ft 2½in (15m); height 14ft 1¼in (4·30m).
**Weights:** Empty (1) 14,748lb (6690kg); normal loaded (1) 23,148lb (10,500kg); maximum loaded (1) 29,762lb (13,500kg).
**Performance:** Maximum speed (1) 345mph (556km/h); (2) 354mph (570km/h); initial climb (1) 2,100ft (650m)/min; service ceiling 33,530ft (10,220m); range (1) 2,728 miles (4390km).
**Armament:** (1 and 2) one 20mm Type 99-II cannon manually aimed from nose, one 20mm or 12·7mm manually aimed from rear cockpit (a few aircraft had dorsal turret with two 20mm or 12·7mm); internal bay for two 551lb (250kg) bombs, plus small bombs beneath outer wings; as alternative, one 1,764lb (800kg) or 1,874lb (850kg) torpedo externally, or

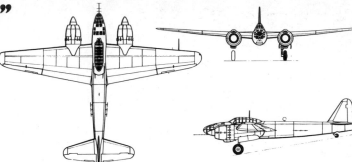

**Above: Three-view of late-model P1Y1 with ASV search radar.**

two 1,102lb (500kg) bombs inboard of engines; (1-S, 2-S) two 20mm fixed firing obliquely upward in centre fuselage, plus single 20mm aimed from rear cockpit, or powered dorsal turret with two 20mm.
**History:** First flight (Y-20 prototype) early 1943; (production P1Y1) August 1943; (prototype P1Y2-S) June 1944
**User:** Japan (Imperial Navy).

**Development:** Similar to late-model Ju 88 aircraft in size, power and capability, this fine-looking aircraft was one of the best designed in Japan during World War II. The 1940 Navy specification called for a land-based aircraft capable of level and dive bombing, but by the time production began at the Nakajima factories at Koizumi and Fukushima it had already become a torpedo bomber, and it was to do much more before its brief career was over. At sea level it could outrun many Allied fighters and it was manoeuvrable and well protected; yet it carried 1,290gal of fuel and had greater range than any other aircraft in its class. Called Ginga (Milky Way), and christened "Frances" by the Allies, this machine would have been a menace had it not been crippled by lack of skilled crews, lack of fuel and lack of spares. Nevertheless Nakajima built 1,002, of which some were used as suicide aircraft while a few were converted into the P1Y1-S night fighter. Kawanishi had meanwhile developed a completely new version, the Kasei-engined P1Y2, and delivered 96 P1Y2-S night fighters called Kyokko (Aurora), which saw little action.

**Below: This photograph appears to show an unpainted development aircraft. All P1Y1s were outstanding aircraft.**

# Yokosuka MXY-7 Ohka "Baka"

## MXY-7 Model 11 and Model 22

**Origin:** Dai-Ichi Kaigun Koku Gijitsusho, Yokosuka; 600 Model 11 built by Dai-Ichi Kaigun Kokusho.
**Type:** Single-seat piloted missile for surface attack.
**Engine:** (11) one three-barrel Type 4 Model 20 rocket motor with sea-level thrust of 1,764lb (800kg); (22) TSU-11 jet engine, with piston-engined compressor, rated at 441lb (200kg) thrust.
**Dimensions:** Span (11) 16ft 4¾in (5m); (22) 13ft 6½in (4·12m); length (11) 19ft 10¾in (6·07m); (22) 22ft 6½in (6·88m); height (both) about 3ft 11¼in (1·20m).
**Weights:** Empty (no warhead) (11) 970lb (440kg); (22) 1,202lb (545kg); loaded (11) 4,718lb (2140kg); (22) 3,200lb (1450kg).
**Performance:** Maximum speed on level (11) 534mph (860km/h); (22) about 300mph (480km/h); final dive speed (both) 621mph (1000km/h); climb and ceiling, normally launched at about 27,000ft (8200m); range (11) 55 miles (88km).
**Armament:** (11) warhead containing 2,645lb (1200kg) of tri-nitroaminol; (22) warhead weight 1,323lb (600kg).
**History:** Start of design August 1944; start of quantity production (11) September 1944; service delivery, early October 1944.
**User:** Japan (Imperial Navy).

**Development:** Having accepted the principle of the Kamikaze suicide attack, the Imperial Navy was only logical in designing an aircraft for this duty instead of using inefficient and more vulnerable conventional machines having less devastating effect. Built partly of wood, Model 11 was carried aloft by a G4M ("Betty"), without bomb doors and specially modified for the task, and released about 50 miles from the target. The pilot then held a fast glide at about 290mph (466km/h), electrically igniting the rocket while pushing over into a steep final dive for the last 30 seconds of trajectory. Though nearly all these missiles failed to reach their objectives, the few that did wrought fearful havoc. Ohka (Cherry Blossom) was called "Baka" (Japanese for "fool") by the Allies, which was not very appropriate. Several manufacturers delivered 755, and 45 unpowered K-1 versions were delivered for training. The Model 22, of which some 50 were delivered, was underpowered. Not completed by VJ-day, the Model 33 would have had the Ne-20 turbojet; Models 43A and 43B were for launching from submarines and land catapults, respectively, but these too failed to see service.

**Right: A genuine operational Model 11, complete with warhead and motor, found abandoned (probably on Okinawa). All Ohka variants carried a cherry blossom motif on the side of the fuselage (here partly obscured by the joint strap).**

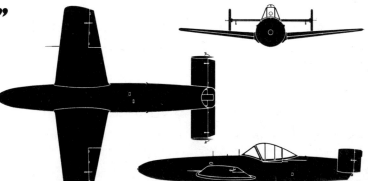

**Above: Three-view of MXY-7 Model 11.**